BOOKS
I READ WHEN I WAS
YOUNG
YOUNG

adol 28, 53, 62, 66,
77, 83, 107, 111, 113,
115, 185

BOOKS
I READ WHEN I WAS
YOUNG

THE FAVORITE BOOKS OF FAMOUS PEOPLE
EDITED BY BERNICE CULLINAN & M. JERRY WEISS

A Project of the Commission On Literature of
the National Council of Teachers of English

AVON
PUBLISHERS OF BARD, CAMELOT AND DISCUS BOOKS

BOOKS I READ WHEN I WAS YOUNG: THE FAVORITE BOOKS OF FAMOUS PEOPLE is an original publication of Avon Books. This work has never before appeared in book form.

Commission on Literature of the National Council of Teachers of English

AVON BOOKS
A division of
The Hearst Corporation
959 Eighth Avenue
New York, New York 10019

Copyright © 1980 by Avon Books
Published by arrangement with the Commission on Literature of the National Council of Teachers of English
Library of Congress Catalog Card Number: 80-68575
ISBN: 0-380-76638-8

First Avon Printing, October, 1980

ACKNOWLEDGMENTS

To the many students, media specialists, and teachers across the nation who responded to the questionnaires to get this project started;

The many publishing companies who were extremely cooperative and encouraging, who assisted us by getting the responses from the many authors included in this volume;

Owen Comora, publicity director, National Broadcasting Company; Jack Blessington, director of Educational Relations, CBS Television; Frank Brady, CBS Television; Pam Warford, director, Community Relations, American Broadcasting Company; Jerry Hellard, American Broadcasting Company;

Nick Naff, Aladdin Hotel; Dave Bradley, Ceasar's Palace; Shelly Miller, Desert Inn; Red McIlvane, Frontier Hotel; Paul Ross, MGM Hotel; Phyllis McCabe, International Hilton; Tony Zoppi, Riviera Hotel; Al Baer, Sahara Hotel; Al Guzman, Sands Hotel; Britt Johnson, Silverbird Hotel; Ron Bell, Sahara Hotel, (all in Las Vegas);

To President William Maxwell; Vice President Joseph Drew, Vice President Edwin Weisman, Jack List and Michael Tepper, Administration and Finance, Jersey City State College;

Susan Costa, Mercedes Diaz, Helen Kiken, Lee Krieg, and Frances Salati for their excellent secretarial assistance, Jersey City State College;

John Shanagher, graduate intern, Jersey City State College;

Sally Hellman, Las Vegas High School, Las Vegas; Eva Bortman, University of Nevada;

Arlene Pillar and Michelle Lagumis, New York University.

PREFACE

How does one define a hero or heroine? *Webster's New Collegiate Dictionary* provides several definitions, but the one most appropriate for this book seems to be "a central personage taking an admirable part in any remarkable action or event; hence a person regarded as a model." When students were asked to name their living heroes, i.e., those they would choose as models, the results predictably reflected a great preponderance of television and rock stars as well as movie and sports figures—that is, people of the media, people who, in some cases, are created by the media. Another type of media figure selected was the politician. In addition, a diversity of writers was chosen.

Some of those named could be categorized as ephemeral heroes. They will be forgotten in five years or less, and others will replace them. On the other hand, some would have been chosen five years ago and might be picked again five years from now. Both types of heroes are valuable. We live in a diverse and changing culture, and the ephemeral hero has a place in providing a temporary model, one which corresponds to the tenor of the times. Humans have a need to belong, to fit within society as it exists. The ephemeral hero helps us fit by creating a common point of reference. Within our altering society we change and grow, and our heroes become different in response to our new needs.

We also have a need for models who remain steadfast, those who represent basic beliefs and values and who transcend time. These heroes are often people who have the courage to be more than mediocre, who become models because of their willingness to be leaders in whatever field they enter. People such as Golda Meir, Albert Einstein, Margaret Mead, Buckminster Fuller, and Frank Lloyd Wright altered society. They are models because of what they represent as humans rather than the particular field of work they chose.

After the heroes were selected by the students in this project, every effort was made to contact each hero named. Each was asked to name three books or authors who had influenced his or her life. The responses were diverse, yet fell in interesting patterns. Many listed books about heroes or those able to meet the challenges of life, including numerous biographies and autobiographies, as well as the Horatio Alger series. Adventure stories were also popular, as were those about nonconformists. *The Adventures of Tom Sawyer, Catcher in the Rye, A Separate Peace,* and *Call of the Wild* were individual titles frequently named. Also, the books of Charles Dickens and Edgar Rice Burroughs were often mentioned. Fantasy had its place, with Tolkien, Jules Verne, and Rudyard Kipling well represented, along with *The Wind in the Willows* and *The Wizard of Oz.*

The fascinating thing about these choices is that many are the same titles chosen today by students in grades six through twelve when they are asked to name three books they would recommend to a friend. *Call of the Wild, A Separate Peace, Catcher in the Rye,* and *The Hobbit* were among the favorites of our current school children.

It would seem that some books, like some heroes, maintain their ability to serve as models for a succession of students in our schools.

M. Jean Greenlaw

INTRODUCTION

The letters from the heroes chosen by students show that books spoke to them in ways we regard as the universal appeals of literature. Some said, "I virtually became the character I read about for a while." Their letters told of play-acting a role, pretending to be the person they read about. Who knows if such role-taking prepared them to become heroes themselves?

Letters from some heroes spoke of childhood as a lonely time—one devoid of playmates. These hero-readers found their friends in books and discovered others like themselves to assure them that they were not alone. Books gave them other lives to live, different worlds to know, and expanded their horizons.

Many spoke of books as motivating forces and shapers of ideals which directly influenced the person they became. They saw the roots of their compassion grounded in the fertile soil of literature, and knew that they had learned what it was to be human through books. Some said directly that books moved them toward humanity, causing them to care about the lives of others. What measure of compassion and caring can we attribute to the books that spoke to today's heroes during their formative years? Such questions cannot be answered with the "skill-to-drill-and-kill" tests used in schools today, but they can be answered with testimony, case studies, and letters from people who have made a difference in our world. This compendium of letters validates the literary experience we want today's students to have. Books made a difference for yesterday's readers who have become today's heroes. We must pass the legacy along by keeping literature alive. Who knows what tomorrow's heroes will have to be? Assuredly they will need personal strength, the conviction of ideals, and compassion—the common ground of literature.

Bernice Cullinan
M. Jerry Weiss

ARNOLD ADOFF

When We Were Very Young by A. A. Milne

Now We Are Six by A. A. Milne

Golden Slippers: An Anthology of Negro Poetry, Edited by Arna Bontemps

Poems by Milne and Robert Louis Stevenson were all around me as a young child. These were the first poems, after *Mother Goose,* to show me the rhythms and music, as well as tell the stories, set the scenes, etc. Milne, especially, opened the musical line and opened my young head to the open form, or free form, poetry I was to encounter as a young student. His poetry has charm and wit and intelligence. It spoke to me directly, even though it came from another country, really another time, than my 1940s childhood in The Bronx, New York. Here was a world beyond New York and being a child of immigrants in New York. And here was a world beyond childhood that still connected with the care and love that I needed.

Golden Slippers was the first collection of Black American poetry I found as an early user of the local branch library. The Bontemps collection hit me in a very youthful and overdeveloped stage of social consciousness. There were few nonwhites in my school classes, and fewer in my social groups. Very little was studied and mentioned in Black American history and literature in classrooms. But I was a student of history at an early age, and full of a young drive to find all answers immediately . . . fit all the pieces of the great puzzle together. If there were many thousands of Black Americans all around me in this city, where was their history, their novels, their poetry, and so on. I came to Black American poetry from politics and the words of Paul Robeson and Vito Marcantonio . . . survivors of the Spanish Civil War. *Golden Slippers* (and other collections by Bontemps and Langston Hughes) gave me my first look at some of the missing pieces of the puzzle . . . some of the first tastes and smells of Black American life as it was depicted by its artists.

These books were vital in my childhood. They also describe the twin forces that take up most of my adult life. Good luck. It is the *combination* of *music* and *meaning* I commend to you. . . .

Arnold Adoff

Jill Gussow

Alan Alda

I read a lot of books as a kid and they were all very different. I think the three that had the strongest effect on me were these:

Top Horse at Crescent Ranch
This was a children's book. I read it when I was eight and I immediately sat down and tried to write my own book about a horse. From then on I knew I wanted to write.

King Arthur and His Knights
I would read myself to sleep at night with the magic of Merlin and the decency and cleverness of the Knights of the Round Table. From then on I knew I wanted to be a magician.

The Congressional Record
For some reason, leather-bound copies of the goings-on in Congress lined the shelves of our living room and I pored over them when I was twelve. I had never read anything so funny. From then on I knew I wanted to do comedy.

Alan Alda

Alan Alda

Choosing only three favorites from the books I read as a child isn't easy! But here are three I dearly loved and still do:

King Arthur and His Knights by Sir Thomas Malory (edited by Philip Schuyler Allen).

Always a bashful, timid boy, I reveled in these bold adventures. True, some were pretty rough, with clashing swords, shattering lances, and a certain njoyousness and high-heartedness. The tales let me glimpse a kind of gallantry and generosity of spirit. Though I tried my best to be as brave as Arthur and his companions, I never quite managed it. But I don't regrt the effort.

The Wind in the Willows by Kenneth Grahame.

When our English teacher was absent, a substitute began reading this book aloud to our class. I was carried away from the first page with Mole, Rat, and Mr. Toad. Fascinated with these animals who behaved like people, I recognized the personality of each one. Their river, their woods were magical places, and, later, helped me to sense the wonders of the real world of nature. The substitute teacher didn't finish the book and neither did I, until nearly twenty years later, when I found it again and finally read it to the end with the same delight I felt as a child.

David Copperfield by Charles Dickens

The people in this book came bursting out of the pages, laughing, shelves of our living room and I pored over them when I was twelvin fact, reminded me of my family, myself included. And what marvelous language! Dickens let me see, smell, and taste his world—and the world itself—as I'd never done before.

Now that I've just finished writing this, I can think of three, and a dozen, others. But I'll let these stand. One thing for sure, the books we love give us something to live on all our lives.

Lloyd Alexander

Lloyd Alexander

Alexander Limont

Mrs. Firnist James Alexander, Sr.

Since I have been reading all my life and cannot remember when I could not read, I have had to stop and think back to my childhood and remember what has truly influenced me most.

As early as eight years of age I began reading the King James Version of the Bible. When I was twelve I won a beautiful chain reference Bible with my name engraved on the leather back. It was a prize for an oratorical contest in which I recited an original essay on Africa. When the Dean of the College presented it to me he said I should read the Bible and let it shape my life and I would have a wonderful life. I think he was right. No other book has influenced me more profoundly.

I began writing poetry the year I was twelve. At ages eleven and twelve I was reading the Black poets of the Harlem Renaissance, and I particularly liked Langston Hughes. I am sure Langston Hughes has also deeply affected my life. All of Afro-American literature has been a part of my life as far back as I can remember. This includes *Crisis* magazine and Dr. W. E. B. DuBois.

Also, at age eleven I entered high school and began studying history and French. Two books that year made an indelible impression upon me. They were the story of the French Revolution with its slogans of freedom, or Liberty, Equality, and Fraternity. I have been deeply concerned with social history ever since. The other book was Victor Hugo's *Les Miserables*. I could not read the French well enough so I read it first in translation and it took a long time. I have never forgotten it.

Finally, but not least, I remember that the year I was twelve my father brought home from his summer's study at Northwestern the one-volume abridged work, Fraser's *The Golden Bough*. That book fascinated me. Little did I realize then its importance for the whole body of western world literature, and especially for T. S. Eliot.

Among the many books I read during my childhood and adolescence I am sure these have influenced me most. All the fairy tales, the Greek myths, tales of Rome, and the poetry that began with *A Child's Garden of Verse* by Robert Louis Stevenson, all of these influenced me, yes, but they are overshadowed by all those mentioned above.

Margaret Walker
Alexander
(Mrs. 7 J.)

Margaret Walker Alexander

THE FLORIDA SENATE

Chip Hilton's sports books

The Adventures of Huckleberry Finn

The Hardy Boys mysteries

Zane Grey books

I am a firm believer in reading for children and if this response is helpful in motivating the students, then I am glad to take the time to provide this information.

Dick Anderson

The poetry of Paul Lawrence Dunbar
    The poems, in both dialect and standard English, contained humor, drama, and tenderness. They helped me to understand the wealth of Black American culture.

A Tale of Two Cities by Charles Dickens
    The drama and love of freedom impressed my young mind. The characters and situations gave me my first vision of England and Europe and helped me to see the similarity in human striving.

Shakespeare's sonnets, and *Hamlet*
The sonnets introduced English lyricism to me. As a young girl I could barely understand the contents, but could easily weep over the beautiful sound of the words read aloud. Hamlet was the first character in a drama with whom I identified. For some reason, I had enormous sympathy for the Melancholy Dane. Possibly because I was melancholy myself.

Joy!

Maya Angelou

Maya Angelou

ARTHUR ASHE

Herewith are my three book choices:

The Bible

African Genesis by Robert Ardrey

Native Son by Richard Wright

Arthur Ashe

The Scottish Chiefs, illustrated by Wyeth

The Story of Ferdinand

Samuel Altsheller books

Ed Asner

A family story insists that at the age of five I appeared at the top of the steps screaming, "I can read! I can read!" What I read no one recalls, but I have never stopped.

The first books I discovered on my own were the many volumes of Thornton W. Burgess: *Blackie the Crow, Sammy the Jay,* and *Lightfoot the Deer.* They and many more became important friends of mine. Cheap, I saved my money and bought as many of these novels as I could and so acquired a library of my own.

Perhaps the most important book I read when I was young was Kenneth Grahame's *The Wind in the Willows.* It had all I desired: deeply felt characters, wonderful adventures, rich comedy, stirring language. At the same time there was something mysterious about the book that moved me greatly. My boyhood copy still sits on my shelf.

I read so much that most has gone from memory. One book gave me something special: Jules Verne's *Twenty Thousand Leagues under the Sea.* Exciting from the start; when I reached the perilous passage under the North Pole I could not—despite the late school night hour—stop reading. Nor did I. I stayed up for most of the night, later than I had ever done before, three or four in the morning until I finished the book.

It may have been the first time I stayed up reading so late, but it was not the last. To my mind there is still no greater pleasure than an exciting book in hand when the rest of the world is asleep. There in the dark I love to voyage far by the light of words!

Rosemary Ranck

Avi

United States Senate
OFFICE OF THE MINORITY LEADER
WASHINGTON, D.C. 20510

Your literacy project is a fine idea, and I am flattered that you have asked for my contribution to it. As a matter of fact, I plan to do my best to increase the role of education in our country. I believe that education lies at the heart of the American experience. It is the engine which, in a climate of freedom, has made possible the upward social and economic mobility which is the hallmark of American history.

You asked what kind of books made the greatest impression on me as a child—and my immediate thought was books about American history and folklore. Were I to list all my favorite authors, this letter might go on for pages.

You have to remember that I was born to a Southern family and a political family. As a result, I was fascinated by authors such as Mark Twain, who brought the American experience in his stories to life in my mind.

Howard H. Baker, Jr.

It is almost impossible to choose only three books which impressed me greatly, because I was a voracious reader. I not only devoured children's books, but at the age of ten, I was raiding my parents' library, which did not always delight them. Also, since I was born in 1923, many of the books that left indelible pictures in my head are no longer in print.

Here's what I will do: I will simply list a panoply of books, and you can choose as you like.

The Goops by Gelet Burgess. *The Twilight of Magic* by Hugh Lofting. Also his *Porridge Poetry* and, of course, his *Doctor Doolittle*. I attacked the King James Version of the Bible with my inner trumpets blowing at the age of eleven and plowed straight through, including the begats and begots. This was not only a feat, but one which prepared me for all language other than our daily spoken American. Poetry of all kinds, and Shakespeare. Frances Hodgson Burnett's *The Secret Garden* and *The Little Princess*. There's always a certain amount of martyr in any pre-adolescent and I identified mightily with both heroines. *The Arabian Nights*, of which I have four different volumes, and both Grimm's and Andersen's fairy tales.

For someone intent on being an actress from the age of three, the magic in all those tales distilled my imagination. A wonderful book by Dorothy Canfield called *Understood Betsy* introduced me, a city child, to country living.

I also loved Charles Lamb's *Tales from Shakespeare*.

I hated *Alice in Wonderland* and was mystified by *The Little Prince* and still believe they are not for children.

Poetry struck me like lightning from an excellent young people's collection by Louis Untermeyer called *This Singing World*—terrific book.

Anne Baxter

The Untouchables

Catcher in the Rye

Portrait of the Artist as a Young Dog by Dylan Thomas

James C. Belushi

James C. Belushi

TONY BENNETT

Crime and Punishment by Dostoevski

The Magic Mountain by Thomas Mann

All books by Charles Dickens

Those authors and books that I read while I was a child influenced me greatly in walking towards humanity, rather than walking away from it. My philosophy of life was also greatly influenced by Pablo Casals, Duke Ellington, and Picasso, all of whom I had the honour of considering friends of mine.

Although I have been a film and stage actor since early childhood, my most rewarding, richest, and most entertaining hours have been those spent absorbed in the miracle of a good book. I love to read.

My high school senior English term paper was on the life and works of John Steinbeck. I spent that entire senior year in Guaymas, Mexico, shooting a film called *Lucky Lady*, and had to do all my school work by correspondence. In the process, I read just about every word Mr. Steinbeck ever published. He is, far and away, my favorite American author. His three books I reacted most strongly to were *In Dubious Battle*, *Of Mice and Men* and *East of Eden*.

Another writer who made a deep impression on me was the English author, A. J. Cronin. I read *The Citadel* when I was eleven years old (in my dressing room while doing a Broadway show), and I return to that inspirational novel periodically, as to an old friend. *Arrowsmith*, by Sinclair Lewis—a book much like *The Citadel*—also impressed me greatly when I read it in junior high school.

Since you asked me to limit my list (I could go on and on), let me add, as a finale, Stephen Crane's *The Red Badge of Courage*. To me, this is the greatest antiwar book ever written. The horror of a Civil War battlefield, that test of a youth's courage—they will be with me always. I read Crane's book when I was thirteen. It changed my whole attitude toward war.

As I said, film and the stage are my life work, but, to me, the greatest movie or play cannot compare to the images I see, the ideas I discover, and the emotions I feel when I'm in the world of a fine book.

Robby Benson

JUDY BLUME

When I was very young my favorite book was *Madeline* by Ludwig Bemelmans. I loved the story and recited it over and over again, pretending that I *was* Madeline. And, of course, I pored over the pictures for hours, each time I brought the book home from the library.

When I was older, in fifth grade, my favorite books were by Maud Hart Lovelace and they were all about Betsy, Tacey, and Tibb and their families. I read the entire series and when there were none left I was terribly disappointed. I liked to daydream about each book and make up my own stories about Betsy.

I think the reason that I remember these books so well is that I identified with the characters in each of them. They were like friends to me.

Judy Blume

Joan Neary

Pat Boone

I've sat for a few minutes trying to remember the books and authors who made an impression on me during my adolescence, and I've really only been able to remember three.

The Adventures of Tom Sawyer by Mark Twain

The Adventures of Huckleberry Finn by Mark Twain

The Bible

I read a great many books, both assigned and for pleasure, but these three loom out of my memory, affecting me pleasurably even now. Sam Clemens, much better known as Mark Twain, had the magical ability to transport you to a time and a place, to help you see and feel and to smell everything in his stories. I felt I knew Tom and Huck and all the others, and the experiences and the images have remained vivid to this day. I believe that the relative innocence of their childhood, with the appealing mischief mixed in, has made millions of us long for simpler days.

I began reading the Bible as a young boy and believed every word. I still do. I read about Jesus as a boy, and came to realize, even in my own childhood and adolescence, that this life was zipping by, and that it was vital I set my priorities even then. I did, on the principles that I read for myself in the Bible. I'm absolutely certain that my life would not have been as blessed with opportunity, material success, wonderful family, and influence for good if it hadn't been for my serious time in the Manufacturer's Handbook while I was in my formative years. How I wish that every young person in America would make it his or her favorite book!

Pat

Pat Boone

bradbury

I cannot name three individual books, but I can name three authors and all of their works which caused me to grow into the kind of writer I have become.

First, L. Frank Baum and his *Oz* books, all of them! I began to read about Oz when I was seven or eight and by the time I was nine I lived, most of the time, in the Emerald City, which seemed a grand place to be, with all my good friends—Ozma, the Tin Woodman, the Scarecrow, Dorothy, and Toto! Mr. Baum taught me how to begin to dream, to fantasize, to have fun with the images inside my mind!

Next came Edgar Rice Burroughs and all of his books about *Tarzan* and *John Carter, Warlord of Mars.* Mr. Burroughs called me out on the lawns of summer at night and told me to reach up my arms and hands and mind to Mars, and he and John Carter would PULL me across Space, forever! I did that. I asked to live in Space for all of my life, and—bang! it happened. I went away to Mars and never came back. My *Martian Chronicles* couldn't have been written, years later, without the Mars of Mr. Burroughs.

Finally, the books of Jules Verne who taught me how to live under the sea, and up in the air, on the way to the moon, and do it with morality, and with good taste and grand fun. His Captain Nemo leads me, even as it led Admiral Byrd to the North Pole.

My best wishes to all of the children living today who will, in the near future, live far out in Space. How wonderful for them!

Ray Bradbury

Ray Bradbury

United States Senate
WASHINGTON, D.C. 20510

The Adventures of Huckleberry Finn by Mark Twain

An Outcast of the Islands by Joseph Conrad

"A Clean, Well-Lighted Place" by Ernest Hemingway

Reading not only is a means of learning, but it provides great entertainment. The wide variety of interests and adventures shared with us by the authors pave the way for our own dreams and aspirations.

Bill Bradley

"ARCHIE BUNKER'S PLACE"

I love to read books, especially Judy Blume books. The reason I love her books so much is that her books deal with real problems kids have and keep to themselves. When you read her books, you realize that you are not alone or different than anyone else. There are other kids dealing with the same problems as you. She teaches you to face the problems, and by doing so you can work them out.

My three favorite books are:

Are You There God? It's Me, Margaret

Tales of a Fourth Grade Nothing

Blubber

I hope the kids who read these books enjoy them as much as I have. Remember, reading books puts you in touch with life and the world.

Danielle Brisebois

Danielle Brisebois

As a child I enjoyed such books as L. M. Montgomery's *Emily* books—*Emily of New Moon, Emily Climbs, Emily's Quest.* I also loved *Rebecca of Sunnybrook Farm,* and the poetry and fairy tales in the Harvard Classics.

However, I read many, many books as a child. There were many kinds in my own home, but there was also a library two blocks away, and *it* was a second home to me.

And I recommend that all of you *read, read, read!* Good therapy, good nourishment—*reliable* nourishment.

Gwendolyn Brooks

Gwendolyn Brooks

As a child I loved books and always had a book to read or to hold. To this day, more than half a century later (!) I still love books and many, many books have made deep impressions upon me.

I grew to love folk tales and poetry above all, and this enthusiasm is still at the heart of all I read.

But in the earliest years, alphabet books and counting books fascinated me most, so I will tell you of these. I discovered that I could not only "read" these books unaided, but that I could also create books like these on my own.

Right off I became the complete author: writing, illustrating, and sewing together the pages of my first alphabet and number books. These limited editions of one were also distributed by me to my parents, relatives, and friends. So you see, way back then I had complete control of the whole book production (I don't now!).

I didn't necessarily wait for the special occasion of a birthday or holiday to present a book, either. If a book were ready at those times, good! Otherwise, any day that a book was "published" became special, and cause enough was found to present it to someone.

That has not changed. To this day, I cannot wait for the proper occasion to present a newly published book. I'm so anxious to share it that I inscribe it for the occasion and send it well in advance. Now, of course, the book production is not limited to one copy; they are printed in the thousands, and I can send the same book to many among my family and friends. But they seem just as happy about that. I think they care only that I still love books as I did as a child, and that I am still making them, with the same excitement, as I did then.

Ashley Bryan

Ashley Bryan

NATIONAL REVIEW

You ask me to name three books that impressed me during my childhood. It is easier to give you the name of three authors. I read the children's books of Robert Louis Stevenson, the *Oz* books by L. Frank Baum, and the *Tom Swift* books by somebody whose name I forget.

Wm. F. Buckley, Jr.

Wm. F. Buckley, Jr.

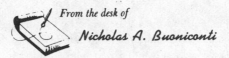

From the desk of
Nicholas A. Buoniconti

The three books I read as a child which made a great impression on me are:

Catcher in the Rye by Salinger

A Tale of Two Cities by Dickens

The Merchant of Venice by Shakespeare

Nick Buoniconti

All Pro Graphics, Inc.

CAROL BURNETT

I love reading, and I loved reading while I was growing up.

Three particular books stand out in my mind because of the beauty of their words, sense of adventure, and the pleasure they gave me.

The first is *The Yearling* by Marjorie K. Rawlings. I cried myself to sleep for weeks after finishing it.

The second is *Jane Eyre* by Charlotte Bronte. Many books circulated for young people when I was growing up centered on males and the relationship of young boys such as Tom Sawyer and Huckleberry Finn. I really couldn't identify with them. When I found *Jane Eyre*, I found a book that had everything to intrigue me, a beautiful story and a strong dramatic plot focused around a young girl and her growth into womanhood.

The third book which influenced me was a gift from my mother. I was interested in becoming a writer, and she presented me with a copy of *Roget's Thesaurus*, which gave me an equal sense of pleasure and adventure. It introduced me to the world of different words for other words with the same or similar meaning.

Carol Burnett

When I was a girl, the first book that I really loved was *The Adventures of Mabel*. It was the first book I ever wanted to own, and I read it again and again. Mabel's life was the way I wanted my own to be—safe and secure and yet filled with very imaginative adventures.

My next love was *Uncle Wiggily Stories*. I got an Uncle Wiggily book every Christmas, and I would search the house all during December until I found it. Then I would read it and wrap it back up. On Christmas morning my mother would say, "Don't you want to read your Uncle Wiggily? I thought you loved Uncle Wiggily."

As I got older, I began to read what my sister was reading. She was older than I, and I wanted to be like her. She introduced me to Margaret Pedler, an English author who wrote romances. My favorite was *Desert Sand*. In this book an Arabian chief falls in love with a young Englishwoman on page two, they are kept apart for the next 397 pages, and on the last page they embrace.

I know that none of these books was on any recommended list or had permanent literary value, and I know I read other more worthwhile, more important books. But these were the books I loved and still remember.

Betsy Byars

Betsy Byars

LOS ANGELES RAMS

I'd be more than happy to share three books I experienced during my childhood.

The Adventures of Huckleberry Finn (eleven years old)

The Miracle Worker (thirteen years old)

Of Mice and Men (fourteen years old)

I think if I had to pick an author it would be John Steinbeck.

John Cappelletti

It is quite an honor and most rewarding to be chosen by many children as a person they most admire. It made me feel like a million.

At the wonderful age of forty-three I am very thankful to all my teachers and members of my family who urged me to read when I was very young. I have never regretted it.

From Hans Christian Andersen to Victor Hugo, my imagination has soared, my emotions served, my mind stimulated, and my life enriched.

I have visited every country in the world, sailed through the roughest sea storms, climbed the highest mountains, met kings and queens, travelled back in time, fought with the greatest of armies, prayed with the greatest of men, and even talked with the animals—all by sitting down and reading a book.

And now for my three books which I believe made an outstanding impression on me during my youth:

A Christmas Carol by Charles Dickens
It made me realize that the love for human beings was more important than the love for money.

The Adventures of Tom Sawyer and *The Adventures of Huckleberry Finn*
They made me realize that I was no different than other children growing up.

The Three Musketeers by Alexandre Dumas

It made me realize that true friendships are the treasures of the world.

Ron Carey

Ron Carey

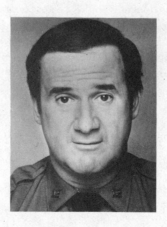

THE WHITE HOUSE

WASHINGTON

This is to acknowledge your letter to President Carter. He is sorry that he cannot answer personally.

While we regret that we are unable to identify for you the President's favorite children's book, we thought you might enjoy the following story about his childhood reading experiences.

In his autobiography, *Why Not the Best?*, the President remarks that his elementary school superintendent, Miss Julia Coleman, prescribed a reading list and awarded him a silver star for every five book reports and a gold star for every ten.

One of those books, selected by Miss Coleman when the President was twelve years of age, was *War and Peace*, by Leo Tolstoy. The President writes that he was at first happy about his choice—because he thought it was about cowboys and Indians—but then was appalled to learn it was 1,400 pages long and not about cowboys at all. However, it turned out to be one of his favorite books, and he has read it two or three times since then.

With the President's best wishes,

Landon Kite

Landon Kite
Staff Assistant

The Autobiography of Malcolm X

The Damned Human Race by Mark Twain

The Grapes of Wrath by John Steinbeck

Thomas Carter

Thomas Carter

Works by John Steinbeck:
Of Mice and Men
The Grapes of Wrath
   It shows how bad it can be, yet we can still go on in one respect or another.

The Scarlet Letter
   Perhaps it shows we all have good and bad in us. Don't look at the surface and don't judge someone by one action.

   Numerous "near-life" fictions by Uris, because within a fictional plot, real life can be seen.

Dave Casper

I read everything that came to hand from the time I was seven or so, and what came to hand was mostly dime novels, traded around with the boys on my block: Horatio Alger, Tom Swift, the Rover Boys, and hundreds of books about Frank and Dick Merriwell at Yale, this last series by Burt L. Standish. My parents were Italian and had no English library. It made no difference to me what I read—any story so long as it moved. These books were most badly written. But all sorts of things were mixed into the batch. In college when I read Swift's *Gulliver's Travels* I discovered I had read it before. On my first reading I did not understand what Swift meant: I read it as a funny story about queer places my first time through.

I also read and could read a lot of Kipling's poetry, especially "The Ballad of East and West." And reams of bad "popular" poetry—"Casey at the Bat," "The Face on the Barroom Floor," and more of that sort were poems I could recite once—and did—often. And there were series of Robert Service. I was a passionate reader but had no one to direct what I read, so I gulped everything. I especially liked poems that told a story—and funny poems. Everything I read jumped off the page and *happened* to me. My pulse ran fast, my temperature went up, my breath grew short. When Mother said "lights out" I hid under the blankets and read on by flashlight to see how it came out.

It would have been better for me, I'm sure, had some adult suggested better books to me, but these certainly filled me with a passion for reading, and I am grateful for that.

John Ciardi

John Ciardi

**FROM THE DESK OF THE CHANCELLOR
UNIVERSITY OF MORATUWA, SRI LANKA**

The book which made the greatest single impression on me (and influenced such novels of my own as *The City and the Stars*) was William Olaf Stapledon's *Last and First Men*. I discovered it in the public library at Minehead (my birthplace) soon after its 1930 publication, so I must have been about fourteen when I read it.

Although the events of this century have departed wildly from Stapledon's scenario, his history of the next two million years, describing the rise and fall of many distinct species of man on several planets until the final extinction of the human race, still remains the most mind-expanding work of science fiction ever written.

H. G. Wells was the second greatest influence, both through his short stories and his novels—above all, *The Time Machine* and *The First Men on the Moon*. Little did I imagine, when I first read the latter, that one day I myself would write the Epilogue to the Apollo astronauts' own narration, *First on the Moon*. . . .

Number three has not been so easy to decide; at first I tried to make a choice between Verne, Conan Doyle, and Rider Haggard, but then I realised that I was being a snob. Third place must go to Edgar Rice Burroughs—who, as chairmen are fond of saying, needs no introduction. . . .

Whatever the literary establishment may say (and I admit that Edgar

Rice Burroughs is virtually unreadable once one is over sixteen), his influence has been enormous—and is, even now, underrated. A writer who can create the best-known character in the whole of fiction is not to be ignored, whatever the deficiencies of his prose style.

Arthur C. Clarke

Billye Cutchen

AMHERST COLLEGE
AMHERST · MASSACHUSETTS · 01002

"*St. Nicholas*" magazine

All the *Henty* novels

Son of the Middle Border by Hamlin Garland

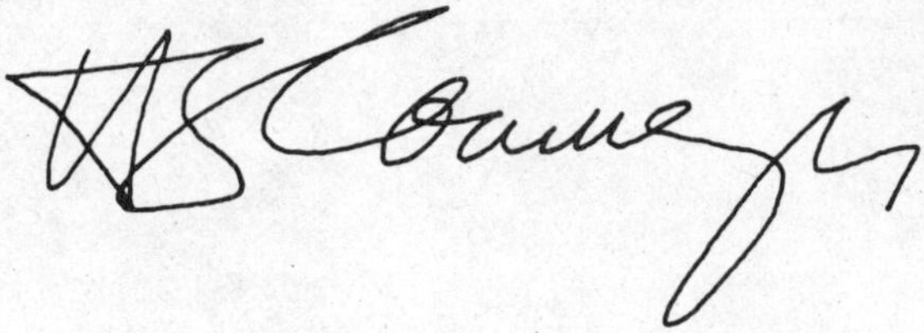

Henry Steele Commager

The three books which made the greatest impression on me during my childhood and adolescence were, in the order of their appearance in my life:

The Adventures of Tom Sawyer by Mark Twain

The Web and the Rock by Thomas Wolfe

The Daring Young Man on the Flying Trapeze by William Saroyan

Each of these books affected me in a different way. But they pointed me in the same direction, toward my eventual destination: becoming a writer. Without these books, my life might have been entirely different from what it is and has been.

Tom Sawyer showed me the drama in the life of a boy—the adventure and the heartbreak that exist in the world of children, including my own childhood. Tom Sawyer made me see the possibility of my own life as the stuff of books: the pangs of a crush on the girl from the other side of town, the longing for adventure, the thrill of midnights in the summertime when the windows were open. Tom Sawyer made me look at my own life for the everyday adventures I might otherwise have missed. He lived out my fantasies. Another thing: *The Adventures of Tom Sawyer* was the first real book I ever owned.

Thomas Wolfe's *The Web and the Rock* confirmed what I already knew in my heart—that I wanted to be a writer. This consciousness had dawned in the seventh grade and never left. It was fortified by Wolfe's novel, which I discovered at the library at the age of thirteen. He expressed what I had felt all along: youth's hunger for knowledge and love and fame; my longing to be a writer and conquer a city like New York. Wolfe told me that someone else out there felt the way I did, that I wasn't alone in my hopes and dreams.

Wolfe's message inspired me, but his style, the way he poured out those mountain torrents of words and phrases and paragraphs, dazzled me. I tried to write like him but was frustrated. I could never summon forth such language, such rhetoric.

And then came William Saroyan. With sentences clear and simple, language that was sweet and direct, Saroyan showed me that one didn't have to write like Wolfe, that there were alternatives. Saroyan freed me from the interminable sentences I had been trying to construct. He proved to me that a clear-running stream could be as effective as a thundering massive river.

I still read these books. They are old friends now. I no longer try to write like Thomas Wolfe or William Saroyan—after thousands of words my own style emerged—but without them or without old friend Tom Sawyer I might never have become a writer.

Robert Cormier

BILL COSBY

Mr. Cosby is out of the office on tour and has asked me to acknowledge your letter. The three books that Mr. Cosby feels influenced him the most are as follows:

The Bible

The Adventures of Huckleberry Finn

Aesop's Fables

Frances L. Shields

Frances Shields
Secretary to Mr. Cosby

Saturday Review

The three books, among many, that I read with deep pleasure and profit in my early teens were:

Lincoln Steffen's autobiography

David Copperfield by Charles Dickens

The Making of an American by Jacob Riis

Norman Cousins

Le Merveilleux Voyage de Nils Holgerson by Selma Lagerloff

Le Livre de la Jungle (The Jungle Book) by Rudyard Kipling

Croc Blanc (White Fang) by Jack London

Jacques-Yves Cousteau

ALEXANDER L. CROSBY

The three most important authors in my early reading years were Thornton W. Burgess, whose animals I still love; Arthur Conan Doyle, who scared me into pulling the curtains when I washed dishes at night; and Jane Austen, who died at forty-two without enriching the world with babes the way she did with books.

Alexander L. Crosby

Kidnapped by Robert Louis Stevenson

The Adventures of Tom Sawyer by Mark Twain

Riders of the Purple Sage by Zane Grey

Norm Crosby

Julia Cunningham

To be asked to name three books that became a part of me is very like crossing over a great meadow where, instead of flowers, all the other books bloom, their pages open to be read. Such a choice means walking past them and pausing to pick just those three, but I'll try.

One that is even now a warmth and a comfort and a delight to me is *The Wind in the Willows* by Kenneth Grahame. The true friendship between the Rat and the Mole has often healed the cuts and hurts that come to anyone, as a child or as an adult. They made me believe, early, that the easy, understanding comradeship they share together through all their adventures, both sad and funny, is quite possible for any of us to find. And this belief, in a moment of loneliness, is enough to erase the dark, to make one very welcome and very happy in their world.

Another is *The Secret Garden* by Frances Hodgson Burnett. This story was an escape for me, a place to be and a place to return to. It was like a piece of music that could be played over and over and always offering the same dramatic wonder and complete satisfaction. To experience the victory of those two unloved and unloving children over neglect and bitterness is a triumph for the reader as well as for them.

For the third I've chosen *The Thirteen Clocks* by James Thurber. Every time I read it, it is fresh, funny, frightening and very beautiful. It is original and surprising. It is and isn't a fairy tale. Above any glittering mountain of praise for this book is the starry fact that in order to stand in front of yourself and look yourself straight in the eyes without flinching you need this book. At least I do.

But I believe, most truly of all, that just opening any book eagerly and allowing the people (or animals) in it to become you is the greatest gift in the world.

Julia Cunningham

Julia Cunningham

Katy Peake

PAULA DANZIGER

The Catcher in the Rye by J. D. Salinger

Pride and Prejudice by Jane Austen

A Separate Peace by John Knowles

"What really knocks me out is a book that, when you're all done reading it, you wish the author that wrote it was a terrific friend of yours and you could call him up on the phone whenever you felt like it.".

Holden Caulfield
The Catcher in the Rye

As an adolescent, I wanted exactly what Holden wanted, to be able to call up the author of certain books. I also wanted to call up the characters created.

Reading about Holden, Gene and Finney, and Elizabeth Bennett helped me become aware that my feelings were not so strange. Others had them also—and since they were allowed to voice these feelings, so could I.

To prepare this response, I reread the three books. I still love them. *Pride and Prejudice* is in many ways the first "young adult novel." Elizabeth saw the world and her family from her own perspective, one filled with humor and growing acceptance and insight.

The Catcher in the Rye, too, is special to me. I so identified with Holden that I read the book every day for over two years during my adolescence. Now I see it from a totally different perspective. Holden is still vivid, alive. Now I can also see his confusion, where once I only felt a kindred spirit.

Finney, in *A Separate Peace*, was alive and special in a way that I wanted to be, creating his own world when his reality wouldn't do.

I've come back to these books at a different point in my life, my mid-thirties. Much of the pain, fear, and anger is gone. My sense of perspective and sense of humor has grown . . . and I still find that these books are special, an integral part of me.

I've come to realize that I can "call" these authors up, that they are "terrific friends of mine." It doesn't take a toll call. . . . All it takes is opening the book and reading it anew.

I hope that all people feel this way about books—and reading.

Paula Danziger

Paula Danziger

Jim Kalett

You ask me to list three books which made a great impression on me during childhood or adolescence. I read constantly during those years, and impressions are hard to sort out, so I will simply name three books that come first to mind:

A Farewell to Arms by Ernest Hemingway

An American Tragedy by Theodore Dreiser

The Collected Poems of T. S. Eliot

I stayed up all one night at my grandmother's house in Sacramento reading *A Farewell to Arms*: I was thirteen or fourteen, and cried and cried when Catherine died.

I read *An American Tragedy* a year or so later, for two straight days, and imagined myself both murdered and a murderer.

I remember the book of Eliot's poems very clearly because it was the first book I ever bought (with a five-dollar gift certificate!), and I memorized all the poems. Again, I think I was thirteen. The cover of that book was pale yellow with very clean black type; I suspect that I bought the book for its cover and came to love the poems after I got it home. Almost everything I read was from the library—the pages had that special cottony feel of library books—and it seemed a tremendous luxury to own this clean and beautiful book.

Joan Didion

Mary Lloyd Estrin

LOIS DUNCAN

The books I loved most as a child were those that contained elements of magic—the whole series of *Oz* books, *Mary Poppins*, *The Princess and the Goblins*—I could name them indefinitely. When I grew up and became a writer, I was told by my editors, "Children today are too sophisticated for books like those. They want to read about real people involved in real situations."

Which was fine, to a point. I did write a number of such books. But the thought kept nagging at me that it would be fun to try to combine both elements, realism and fantasy, and write about forms of magic which might actually exist in today's world. My first attempt at this was *A Gift Of Magic*, about a girl with ESP. When that proved successful, I went a bit further and tried a supernatural gothic, *Down a Dark Hall*, and a book about Ozark witchcraft, *Summer of Fear*. With each of these books, it was like reaching back into my own youth to please the child I used to be.

In my teens I became enchanted with the love poems of Edna St. Vincent Millay. She and I were both hopeless romantics, and I started writing poems as much like hers as I could make them. I was horrified in college to discover that English professors looked down their noses at Edna. I loved her—and still do.

In my later teens I discovered a whole world of mystery novels and psychological suspense stories and began gobbling them up at the rate of one a day. I can't come up with one specific title that was outstanding—it was the idea that as soon as I finished one there was another waiting to be read that was so exciting.

What this all adds up to, I guess, is that there were no three special books that influenced my life—it was *reading itself*—the knowledge that I need never be lonely or bored or feel left out of things because there were books to echo my every mood and fill every need. Books were such an important part of my life that from early childhood on I knew that someday I was going to write them myself.

Lois Duncan

Lois Duncan

JEANNETTE H. EYERLY

Three books which made a great impression on me as a child, and which I read over and over again, are:

Little Women by Louisa May Alcott

The Adventures of Tom Sawyer by Mark Twain

The Secret Garden by Frances Hodgson Burnett

There were, of course, others, but the three I've listed were the first to come to mind.

None of these books was "new" when I was a child, and I doubt that the passage of more than fifty years has dimmed their charm for today's young readers. I envy them making the acquaintance of Jo and her sisters, Tom and Huck and Colin and Mary—they are *such* good friends of mine!

Jeannette H. Eyerly

Jeannette H. Eyerly

Audrey Flack

In searching my mind I found that the greatest literary impression made on me was a poem—"Invictus" by Wm. Ernest Henley. Although I do not remember the anthology it was published in, I have memorized the poem and recently used it on a plaque in a recent painting of mine which is now in the Milwaukee Museum. This poem indicated to me at an early age that I could be "the master of my fate, the captain of my soul."

The other, oddly enough, is a verse set to music—"The Lost Chord."

The third is the entire *Nancy Drew* series, from which I derived great pleasure and imagery.

Audrey Flack

Jeanne Hamilton

GERALD R. FORD

In my opinion, the ability to read rapidly and well is one of the greatest assets anyone can acquire. Not only does a love of reading open unlimited worlds of adventure, but it unlocks the doors to business success.

The books I recall making a deep impression on me were the Horatio Alger series. As a boy, I devoured every one of them. While I was enjoying the individual stories, I also marveled over the successes made by boys who were not so different from me.

Gradually, I absorbed the truth that there are almost no limits to the goals a person can reach with faith in himself and in God, a willingness to work toward those goals with determination, and the perseverance to rise and try again when a defeat knocks you to your knees.

I cannot over-emphasize the fact that the ability to read is well worth any amount of time or effort it may require to achieve.

Gerald R. Ford

Gerald R. Ford

Official Photograph
The White House
Washington

Alan Dean Foster

I always wanted to travel. But it's tough when you're small. For some peculiar reason adults don't believe children should do much traveling. Or they don't have the time to help them, or the means.

There's another way. Through books. A book can take you to the depths of the oceans, the peaks of the Himalayas, the ends of the universe, the ends of time. So I did my early traveling through books.

Three you asked for and three I give you, though I could as well name three hundred.

The Lost World by Arthur Conan Doyle
This is still my favorite book.

Moby Dick by Herman Melville
In my opinion, the best American piece of fiction ever written. Enthralling then and now.

The Golden Nature Guides
I list these together, because they really belong as one. Pieces of the Earth, they introduced me to the colors of the world, its smells and

sights, all the flavor of nature, and this glorious globular spaceship we drift through eternity upon.

Open your eyes, let your minds reach forth, and grasp at these and every other clump of printed matter you can find. They will excite you, teach you, entertain you.

Reading is Freedom.

Alan Dean Foster

I loved to read as a youngster—and I continue to read voluminously. To pick *three* books is hard to do, but . . .

I romantically read and reread *The Secret Garden*.

I was enthralled with *Gone with the Wind*.

And I still cry when I read Oscar Wilde's *Fairy Tales*—particularly "The Happy Prince."

Bonnie Franklin

Photo Division
CBS Television Network Press Information

My favorite childhood books by far and away were the *Mother West Wind* series by Thornton Burgess. I was able to pass my series along to my son when he was six and seven, and he enjoyed them also. Reddy the Fox and old Granny Fox are still two of my favorite characters.

I am also a Robert Louis Stevenson fan. I loved his poetry and in fact still do. "Green leaves afloating/ Castles on the foam/ Boats of mine go boating/ Where will all come home?" That's just a stanza, but it remains a valid question to me as an adult.

My parents purchased for my sister and me an encyclopedia called *The How and Why* which included among its volumes a literature volume. I loved and still love the poetry and short stories. "The Gingham Dog and the Calico Cat" (don't you just see the Iranian crisis in that?); "Winkin, Blynkin and Nod;" Christina Rossetti's "Rainbows"—"Boats sail on the rivers/Ships sail on the seas/ But the clouds that sail across the skies are prettier far than these./ There are bridges on the rivers/As pretty as you please/But the bow that bridges heaven/ And overtops the trees/ And builds a road from earth to sky are prettier far than these." I hope I am doing justice because I am quoting from memory.

Nikki Giovanni

Nikki Giovanni

GRANT M. GOODEVE

The three books that meant the most to me in my youth, and still mean a great deal to me, are:

Le Petit Prince (The Little Prince) by Antoine de Saint-Exupéry

The Wind in the Willows by Kenneth Grahame

Something Wicked This Way Comes by Ray Bradbury

Grant Goodeve

Grant M. Goodeve

Robert Guillaume

Silas Marner by George Eliot

Manchild in the Promised Land by Claude Brown, Jr.

Great Expectations by Charles Dickens

As there will be children reading this letter, I would like to encourage each and every one of them to do as much reading as possible. To read well is one of the most important skills that you will ever learn, and it's one that you will use every day of your life. There's no end to the excitement, the knowledge, and the challenges that reading books can provide for you. And, each time that you pick up a book and read, you'll grow a little more inside.

I want to wish each one of you the very best from all of us at "Benson." And remember, keep reading. . .

Robert Guillaume

I recall a book entitled *There was Once a Slave*, written by Shirley Graham (Du Bois), about the life of Frederick Douglass, who had the foremost voice in the abolitionist movement of the nineteenth century. At the time (1948) and as a teenager, I knew nothing of Douglass or Ms. Graham, but I did often search for material having to do with blacks — I suppose because my own extended family was such a force in my life. Graham's book about this great orator and former slave seemed to speak to me particularly, since my own ancestors had been fugitives from bondage. After this book was published, Ms. Graham married Dr. W. E. B. DuBois, whom I would years later write a biography....

I learned from the Graham biography of Douglass that real human beings could be brought to life through words, as well as the history of the times in which they lived.

As an adolescent, I enjoyed the adventures of Nancy Drew, the heroine from the series of that title. My memory is that these books had for me the excitement of problem-solving. Nancy Drew was a young woman who always took the initiative, and I appreciated that about her. To this day, I don't clearly remember a single story. But the flavor of them remains with me.

The last book was a huge fairy tale book given to me at Christmas when I was much, much younger. There were full color illustrations of Cinderella and her beautiful ball gown full of stars. To a child such as myself, it was lovely. I longed to be her, accepting the hard work in order to reach the reward. There's a moral there!

Virginia Hamilton

Virginia Hamilton

Susan Hirschman

phillies
NATIONAL LEAGUE
EASTERN DIVISION CHAMPIONS

I'm honored that I have been chosen by numerous children as a person they admire. I seem to have a mutual admiration for children, maybe because they are my size. Anyway, let's get to the business at hand.

During my childhood I wasn't much of a reader; in fact, I didn't enjoy it at all. I was always more interested in sports. Reading was something I had to do to get through school. Not that much sticks out in my mind when it comes to books or authors. I do remember enjoying Pearl S. Buck and James A. Michener.

I'm now thirty-five years old and am just getting into reading. It's become a great source of entertainment, relaxation, and knowledge. I guess it's true—you are never too old to learn.

Bud Harrelson

ONE DAY AT A TIME

Early in life I was always partial to the historic narrative. My first memorable reading experience was my involvement with *Ivanhoe* by Sir Walter Scott. All the significant events of the day were in some way touched by this fellow.

I carried this preference right through high school and on into college. My freshman year at Fordham was almost entirely devoted to the reading and rereading of *The Captain from Castile* by Samuel Shellabarger. Again, the great surge of momentous events . . . just loved it!

Finally, let me tell you my most beloved grand narrative. It wasn't even a novel, but rather a poem; "Evangeline" by Henry Wadsworth Longfellow. I read it ten or eleven times and cried and triumphed each time. It was my first love and in some ways my most passionate. Read it, you'll never forget it.

Read on, kids!

Pat Harrington

nat hentoff

When I was very young, I discovered Andrew Lang's series of fairy tales. Each book had a different color. There was the Crimson Fairy Book, the Green, Blue, Lilac, Olive, and on and on. I think I read every one, some of them more than once, because these stories were so full of wonder. I mean wondrous people and events, and wondrous acts of courage and faithfulness to ideals. Through these books, any time I wanted to, I could leave my home and my neighborhood and indeed my century and journey to all sorts of astonishing places. I learned, in short, that books were magical and that, through them, I could forget all those daily things in my world that pressed in on me, and instead I could choose from scores of other worlds.

When I was somewhat older, I came upon Lewis Carroll's *Alice in Wonderland* and *Through the Looking Glass*. These were even freer flights of imagination, and what I especially loved were how the words came alive—how the words themselves could change shapes. How playful they could be, and how funny. So from Lewis Carroll, I especially learned how wondrous language itself is.

Then, when I was fifteen or so, I read a novel, *Darkness at Noon*, by Arthur Koestler. But it read as if it were true—and I later found it really was. The book was about Russia under Stalin, but it could be about any country frozen in the control of one man or a group of rulers who feared dissent, who feared free thoughts, more than anything in the world. It was a frightening book, more so than any of the horror stories I used to read in pulp magazines, but it was also tremendously exciting because it got me to actually understand why freedom of thought and of speech was the basis for all other freedoms. I suppose some of my teachers had told me these things in school, but it took a book—a book by a powerful storyteller—to awaken me to what has become a life-long passion for free expression, including the right of those thoughts I hate to be as freely expressed as my own.

Nat Hentoff

Harold Strauss

ISABELLE HOLLAND

Little Women by Louisa May Alcott

This was given to me when I was about nine by my mother, who thought an American child growing up in England should know something about American literature, history, and background. Of all books I read as a child, this is the one that probably meant most to me over the longest period. I read and reread it—to the point where I read nothing else for about two years and could tell you in exactly what context any line quoted from the book came. I then read the other Alcott books and enjoyed them, though not with the same overwhelming sense of living in their world.

Alice in Wonderland and *Alice Through the Looking Glass*

Another favorite, originally read to me by my mother. I loved the humor of the situation—that is, of a child with no humor at all in a fantastic dreamlike series of events to which she responded with literalmindedness.

Anne of Green Gables

I read and adored the whole series—and reread most of them. Again, they became a world which totally blotted out everything else. For long periods of time Prince Edward Island off the Canadian coast was infinitely more real to me than Lancashire, England, where I happened to be living.

The Milne books

Also read to me at first by my mother—after read by myself. Again the sense of a world into which I could move when I read, and again the warm, gentle humor. I always totally identified with Pooh Bear, because of his tendency to think about food and his equal tendency to get into trouble. There were times, though, that I felt more like Piglet.

The William books by Richard Crompton

Not known over here. William, who was about ten or eleven, and his three friends, Ginger, Henry, and Douglas, got into one adventure-mishap after another, and were a constant source of anxiety to William's mother—Mrs. Brown. I adored the books. The nearest American equivalent I can think of are the books of Beverly Cleary.

David Blaize and David of Kings by E. F. Benson (written about 1919)

E. F. Benson is known over here for his Lucia books. The two David books were about David's school years and then his three years at King's College, Cambridge. And they were about the relationship between David, who was thirteen at the opening of the book and just beginning his public (private, boarding) school, and Frank Maddox, who at the opening is seventeen and also goes on to Kings. I was much too innocent to realize the full implications of such a relationship—although I hasten to add that the author was clear enough that this was a sort of hero-worship and crush only on the part of David, who was in no way attracted by any more intimate relationship. Frank, though, who saw the danger and had experienced it with others, was influenced to draw back by David himself. This book would be impossible to give to a teenager of either sex today. The various warnings against homosexuality would infuriate today's gays, and the whole thing has a cautionary tale quality that wouldn't go down at all well. Yet the books had a vivid story, a lot of humor, a lot of charm and were tremendously popular when I was growing up. I often wonder just how much of *The Man without a Face* grew out of them. . . .

Countless historical novels by such writers as Stanley Weyman and Rafael Sabatini

I was almost a little embarrassed by my early passion for historical novels, until I heard Barbara Tuchman, who was also pooh-poohing them, suddenly stop in mid-sentence and admit that it was her childhood love of historical novels that led to her love for history.

*I reread the David books not long ago. They're still terrific. . . .

lee bennett hopkins

It seems quite odd, being a writer and prolific reader, that I didn't develop a love for books as a child. I did so as an adult. The first six years of my professional life were spent as an elementary school teacher in New Jersey. It was then that I realized how truly important books are.

Three books that do strongly stand out in my mind, however, books that made great impressions during my growing-up years, were:

The Five Hundred Hats of Bartholomew Cubbins by Dr. Seuss

Little Women by Louisa May Alcott

Mama's Bank Account by Kathryn Forbes
  (I must have had good taste in that all three are still quite popular!)

I came across *The Five Hundred Hats* . . . when I was very young. (The book was published in 1938, the year I was born!) From then on I was hooked on Dr. Seuss, an author whom I have had the rare privilege of interviewing several times.

During my teenaged years, I read and reread *Little Women* and *Mama's Bank Account*—wonderful books about families and their struggles for survival.

Perhaps these novels left more of a mark on me than I ever realized. Perhaps that is why my own first novel, *Mama*, portrays a family who has to overcome hardships in their own way.

I wish you luck and love and that your life be filled with wonderful books. There is nothing—no thing—better in the world than reading. Happiness. . .

Lee Bennett Hopkins

Misha Arenstein

The Catcher in the Rye by J. D. Salinger

Look Homeward, Angel by Thomas Wolfe

The Great Gatsby by F. Scott Fitzgerald

Ken Howard

Photo Division
CBS Television Network Press Information

"*Breakfast of Champions.*"

My three favorite books as a child were:

The Babe Ruth Story

The Adventures of Tom Sawyer

An autobiography of Jim Thorpe

These books told the story of men with admirable traits, and had somewhat influenced me as a child.

I hope children today will take the time to do some reading, and perhaps become inspired to take on challenges and strive for excellence in a particular area due to something they have read.

Bruce Jenner

As a young girl growing up in Phoenix, Arizona, I enjoyed reading at an early age. My grandfather used to buy my sister and me beautiful books to read.

Actually, instead of toys he would buy us books. So I began to enjoy reading at the age of five years. Some of the books that I remember so well were:

The Adventures of Tom Sawyer by Mark Twain

The Hobbit by Tolkien

Hans Christian Andersen's *Fairy Tales*

Alice in Wonderland by Lewis Carroll

Dr. Seuss books

I must say that reading books as a child helped stimulate my imagination as an actress. Where else can you travel to far-away lands and experience feelings of other characters by the flip of a page?

Yes, television can be fun to watch, but I still think books are Number One!

Dianne Kay

Dianne Kay

I've enjoyed having the opportunity to recollect my favorite books from childhood. I haven't been able to remember all of the authors, but hope that this partial list will be helpful:

Grimm's Fairy Tales

Andersen's Fairy Tales

The *Bobbsey Twins* series by Laura Lee Hope

Mary Poppins books

The Five Little Peppers and How They Grew by Margaret Sidney

Betsy, Tacey and Tib and all the books by Maud Hart Lovelace

The *Nancy Drew* books by Carolyn Keene

The *Hardy Boys* books

Little Women by Louisa May Alcott

A Child's Garden of Verses by Robert Louis Stevenson

Winnie the Pooh by A. A. Milne

Alice in Wonderland by Lewis Carroll

The Adventures of Tom Sawyer by Mark Twain

The Adventures of Huckleberry Finn by Mark Twain

It also seems to me that I began reading some of the books by Charles Dickens when I was in junior high school, and enjoyed them very much, particularly *Oliver Twist*.

Linda Kelsey

Linda Kelsey

United States Senate
WASHINGTON, D.C. 20510

Thank you for giving me the opportunity to participate in your effort to inspire young people to do more reading. I certainly agree that reading is not only a pleasurable but also an educational experience. It is important for young people to know that television and movies do not, and cannot, take the place of reading. Reading not only expands one's knowledge, it also helps develop vocabulary and writing skills, and helps expand our imaginations.

As a child, there were many books I enjoyed reading. I remember before I could read by myself, my mother read from *Black Beauty* by Anna Sewell before I went to sleep. Later, when I was older, I remember reading *Treasure Island* by Robert Louis Stevenson which I enjoyed enormously, and also *A Tale of Two Cities* by Charles Dickens. These are just three of the many books I enjoyed reading as a youth, and I hope today's young readers will enjoy these and other books suggested by the Literature Commission.

Edward M. Kennedy

BERNIE KOPELL

Isn't it ironic that someone made prominent by the "monster," commercial television, should be thought of so highly by youngsters, the supposed "victims" of its corrupting and de-intellectualizing powers? I feel it is very important that I say to children, even though my professional life is spent almost solely on commercial television, that although TV seems to be the easiest, most accessible, most stimulating medium, if not used moderately and with some judgment it can "turn our brains to mush." Already people are talking about the average person's seven-minute attention span, because so many of us were conditioned on TV, and after seven minutes we've been consistently interrupted by "a word from our sponsor," which by now means something like three to five commercials. To compound the injury, the producers, realizing that all these interruptions make the "story" harder to follow, have simplified the story, made it less subtle, told it with "broader strokes," so when our audience comes back, after the beer, soap, undies, pizza, soft drink pitch, it can easily slide right back to what is left of the plot.

Okay, so much for biting the hand that feeds me. Let me tell you of very thrilling events in my young life.

James Michener is an author who has spoken to me with great force at different times as I've grown up. When I read the *Fires of Spring* during my adolescence, it was as though he was explaining to me the things I was feeling about growing up, a first awareness of my new feelings, desires, the evolving of my manhood, and all the wonders that had just opened up to me, and the wonders beyond that held the promise of opening up. Wow! Television never was that exciting.

The same author's *Hawaii* which I read before I ever visited those beautiful, perfumed, gently blowing islands, with his almost Biblical description of Hawaii's birth. Hawaii literally exists now where nothing but water existed for millions of years. The islands were formed by a number of volcanic eruptions. It's very likely that the first eruptions reached the surface, one heaving forth of the earth through the water, building on the last until this magnificent island chain was created. Michener describes this in a way that can take the top of your head off! And then he tells of the people who came, first the early Polynesians from the older existing islands of Tonga, Samoa, Bora Bora,

New Hebrides, etc., and later, the Portuguese, Chinese, Japanese, and New Englander missionaries. When I went to Hawaii for the first time in 1970 I had the advantage of having read his book. My appreciation was made deeper because I had more information and background. The islands make me happy just about once every year, and I'm always grateful to Mr. Michener.

For my third book, how about *Vanity Fair* by William Makepeace Thackeray. There is a reference in Shakespeare to "the gentle parts of speech." People of a century or so ago were not as "direct" as we are today. They took longer to say things. Words were very important. Letters between lovers were exchanged a great deal. Love letters were written frequently, written and saved and cherished. It was a time when people seemed to be in love with *words*, differing tremendously from today, when the *image* or the *moving picture* is the thing. People used words as the tools of imagination, so that the image that they were trying to convey was created in the minds of the reader. Scholars argue that that way our imagination can soar without bounds and our image of today is limited by what we are shown on our television screens at home or movie screens in the theater.

I'm grateful for this opportunity to express myself to youngsters. It's very important that the people children see on television are not thought of as related exclusively to the "boob tube."

Bernie Kopell

Bernie Kopell

Three of the books I read and enjoyed very much during my earlier years were:

Treasure Island by Robert Louis Stevenson

Kim by Rudyard Kipling

The Count of Monte Cristo by Alexandre Dumas

I liked these books because all are rattling good adventure stories, the first a story of buried treasure and pirates with characters that are alive and exciting. I can still hear the creak of the old sign above the Admiral Benbow Inn, and the rattle of horses' hoofs on the frozen road the night they ran down Old Pew, and the thump of Long John Silver's peg-leg.

Kim is the story of espionage in India, of the secret ways of travel for those involved in it. Here was an underground before the word became popular—the old lama, their fat and wily friend, and the mysterious happenings along the Great Trunk Road of India. Many years later I travelled that road myself, by bicycle and on foot. It had changed but little.

The story of the escape from Chateau d'If has to be one of the great escape stories of all time, and then how the Count returned to Paris to get revenge on those who had falsely accused him and lied to send him to prison. All three are great stories, exciting stories, but they do more: each one introduces you to chapters of history that might be no more than lines in a history book. The whole story of the Spanish Main comes alive in *Treasure Island*, British India in *Kim*, and France of the time during and after the Revolution in *The Count of Monte Cristo*.

There are dozens of others I enjoyed as much. *Scaramouche* by

Sabatini, *Johnny Tremain* by Forbes. I also read a great many books by G.A. Henty, all historical novels no longer available, and the Joseph A. Altscheler books of the Civil War and the Revolution.

Once one discovers how much fun it can be to read, one's life is never dull, and the interest grows with each book. Places you have never seen are known to you and are real, and you can walk in times far from yours, and when you wish you can speak to the great minds of all ages. I sit, as I write this, in the midst of an 8,000-volume library of my own, and it is Aladdin's Cave. I can at will move into any time in history; I can talk with the great minds of the past, with philosophers, outlaws, cattlemen, adventurers, with kings, queens and common sailors. It is all here, waiting for me. In any bookstore or public library, it waits, too, for you.

Louis L'Amour

Louis L'Amour

NANCY LARRICK

One of my favorite books as a child was *Nights with Uncle Remus: Myths and Legends of the Old Plantation* by Joel Chandler Harris. Almost every night my father read me stories from this book of animals that talked and behaved like people. I loved Brer Rabbit and was thrilled to hear how he outwitted the fox and the bear and the wolf. Later I found it was not an easy book for me to read because it is written in Southern dialect, but I was captivated by the sound of language as my father read it aloud to me.

Another favorite was *The Wonder Book* by Nathaniel Hawthorne, which was given to me by my godmother. It was beautifully illustrated in color. As I read the story of King Midas or the tale of Pandora's Box, I drank up every detail of those glorious pictures. One of my great regrets is that this book got lost in my moving around since childhood.

I think my favorite author was Lucy Fitch Perkins, who wrote the Twins books, dozens of them. I must have read every one that our library owned. My two favorites were those I owned, *The French Twins* and *The Belgian Twins*, which I read over and over. The line drawings in those books were so true to the scenes of Paris and Brussels that I remembered them vividly when I visited those cities years later.

Nancy Larrick

Nancy Larrick

Stuart Little by E. B. White

Doctor Doolittle by Hugh Lofting

Island Stallion by Walter Farley

Linda Lavin

THE PRESIDENT'S COUNCIL ON PHYSICAL FITNESS AND SPORTS
WASHINGTON. D.C. 20201

Your request is both flattering and most difficult. Flattering in that my so-called athletic achievements were a generation ago, although I am still actively coaching divers (fancy) on weekends and on my vacations. Difficult because I must recall those glorious days of reading some forty-five to fifty years ago! I shall try.

Dr. Doolittle's stories were eagerly read, and whenever a new story showed up on the bookshelf I would take it out. How I used to hope that we humans could talk to the animals. How I wondered why we did not show the faith and friendship those animals did to us, no matter how much we hurt them with our stupidity.

Zane Grey's story of the West, and Edgar Rice Burrough's *Tarzan of the Apes*. They allowed me to fantasize how good conquered evil, with the fast gun used only to right a wrong. Tarzan was the man who could outswim crocodiles, conquer gorillas, etc. Man against all odds through personal strength could do all those wonderful things in the name of justice and fair play.

Sammy Lee, M.D.

Sammy Lee

P.S. I have been a member of the above Council since 1979. I started with President Nixon, then President Ford, and now with President Carter. Standing some five feet one and a half inches, I am the shortest but longest member of the fifteen-member Council.

As a lonely only child growing up in New York City, I read a great deal, so it is very difficult to list only three books and three authors. One of my favorites was *Emily of New Moon* by L. M. Montgomery, and the two books following it, of *Anne of Green Gables* fame. While I enjoyed the "Anne" books, Emily meant a great deal more to me because she, too, wanted to be a writer. She also had gifts in what we would now call parapsychology, and her ability to break through the limited barriers of ordinary living also appealed to me and helped me to widen my own horizons.

I also read, and reread, the works of E. Nesbitt, that amazingly liberated nineteenth-century lady—both the family books about the Bastable children and her fantasies. Since I was an only child, the delightful give and take between the Bastable children was particularly appealing to me. For many years at Christmas my only two requests were for an older brother and an elephant, and I could never understand why I didn't get either. The Nesbitt fantasies, again, opened a wider world than the limited world of provable fact in which the school child is often stuck. Intuitively, I knew that there was more to it than that.

For my third author I will list Oscar Wilde and his poignant fairy tales.

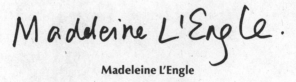

Madeleine L'Engle

Although I read widely and intensely during childhood, there aren't any authors or books which made a great impression on me. Perhaps this is because of my racial background, and there simply weren't books which spoke to my reality as a black child growing up in a hostile white world. So while I read widely in the areas of history, geography, and biography, no books or authors stand out as important now.

I do recall, however, that my important reading was crime magazines, comic books, and detective novels, namely Perry Mason. My only explanation for the importance of these reading materials is that they helped mitigate the violence which was a part of my immediate environment.

It was not until I entered college that my reading matter became more serious—which leads me to wonder if what a child reads is less important than the act of reading itself. At least such would seem to be true in my life.

Julius Lester

Julius Lester

SAM LEVENSON

My adolescent reading was not concerned with the realities of my ghetto life but with the great world beyond. *The Microbe Hunters* brought me into the world of scientific curiosity; Schindler's *Life of Beethoven* convinced me that even the deaf could hear the sounds of greatness. Irving Stone's life of Van Gogh got me to feel visually.

These men brought me a true picture of men created in the image of God.

Sam Levenson

Diana Bryant

I am terrible at lists. There were so many books from my childhood that I loved and still love that narrowing it down to three seems like an impossible task. However, here goes.

Alice in Wonderland was and is one of my favorite books. I read it again and again when I was a child. I had a set of *Alice in Wonderland* dolls, and I used to make up plays and pretend I was all the characters. I find that book as magical today as I did when I first read it.

I loved almost all the *Black Stallion* books by Walter Farley. I loved horses, and I used to go to sleep telling myself the Black Stallion stories, only I got to play Alex. Interestingly, the one Walter Farley book that I remember the best was *Island Stallion.* Since that book was about a red horse, and I married a redhead, I'd have to say it definitely made a lasting impression.

I think that at one time in my life I had read every *Nancy Drew* book. In some ways, Nancy, Bess, and George are as vivid to me today as they were when I was nine years old. Although I do not reread the *Nancy Drew* books as an adult, I believe they started me on a lifelong addiction to reading and writing mysteries.

As you can see, I cheated. Two of my selections are series, so I managed to mention more books than three. But any list of my favorite books whether from childhood or as an adult has to include *Little Women, The Secret Garden, Treasure Island, Mary Poppins,* and *Pippi Longstocking.* I warned you I was terrible at lists.

Elizabeth Levy

Elizabeth Levy

Henry Gordillo

The Touchstone Center For Children, Inc.

Now We Are Six by A. A. Milne

The Fields, The Trees, and *The Town* by Conrad Richter

The Wanderers by Alain Fournier

   These books represented the ways in which reading can bring us closer to distant worlds as well as to the roots of our immediate experience.

R. lfK

Richard Lewis

The three books that made the greatest impression on me back in the days when books could make a great impression on me were:

The Royal Road to Romance by Richard Halliburton

This was my introduction to the author as hero; first you swim the roiling, croc-infested waters, then you write about it. Since I wasn't sure at the time whether I wanted to grow up to have adventures or write about them, this book solved my problem. I could do both!

Cannery Row by John Steinbeck

This was my first Steinbeck novel. His compassion for people, his sense of place, and his love for nature overwhelmed me. I read all his books, often twice in a row. Although I never tried to emulate his style or subjects, he became my role model as a writer.

Catcher in the Rye by J. D. Salinger

I read this book when I was fourteen. It was a portable support group. Here was a character, intelligent, sensitive, real, who was crazier than I was. But only by degree. And he was speaking directly to me.

Good luck in finding your own special books.

Robert Lipsyte

Listed below are the three books which I most enjoyed as a child. I hope that the children will find them as exciting as I did.

Mutiny On The Bounty

Treasure Island

Swiss Family Robinson

George Lucas

Enterprises, Inc.

Loretta tells me that she really has no recollection of any readings at an early time in her life. When you only go as far as the fourth grade, you don't pick up reading habits, good or bad.

The first book that she does recall reading and having a lasting impression of is the Bible, in her late teens and early twenties.

Then, for the past several years, she has become an avid reader of historical literature.

David Skepner
Executive Vice President

MARY B. Mac CRACKEN

The books which made the greatest impression on me were:

The Secret Garden by Frances Burnett

Lassie

All the Albert Payson Terhune books

—and later on—

Ethan Frome by Edith Wharton

I also spent many wonderful hours in the tiny public libraries of Tenafly, New Jersey, and in the summer, Hammond, New York.

I was allowed to pick out seven new books each week—and each seemed like a special gift!

Mary MacCracken

Mary MacCracken

Three of the books which made strong, really stunning, impressions upon me as a teenager were Richard Wright's *Black Boy*, Willard Motley's *Knock on Any Door*, and Betty Smith's *A Tree Grows in Brooklyn*. Two of the authors, Wright and Motley, are Black. Ms. Smith is white.

Ms. Smith's chief character, Francie Nolan, was as real to me as the poems I was then scribbling. Francie's hopes and dreams were so much like my own; her life paralleled mine. I saw the struggles of my mother, Alice Frazier Bell, in Kathy Nolan (Francie's mother). My father, John "Red" Bell, like Francie's father (Johnny Nolan), was a wonderful singer who never got the break he deserved. My father sang at countless weddings, funerals, churches, and small clubs in Atlantic City and New York. Under the auspices of the WPA, my father sang—for more than a year—each Tuesday and Saturday, over WFPG (a radio station in Atlantic City). Francie's father was a singing waiter. My father was also a singing waiter (at the Dude Ranch in Atlantic City). When Francie's father died his awful death, I was shattered. Was my father unhappy too? Would he also give up?

In the poignant world spun by Wright and Motley, I saw myself, my family, my friends, my neighbors—and all of our foes—magnified a zillion times! These two Black writers (as well as other Black authors whose works were not only welcome but treasured in my home) took me, a Black and sensitive youngster, where only a Black writer could. They allowed me to believe that I, too, could write, could create. They nourished my imagination. Through their words, I grew up whole and healthy. They were magnificent teachers who taught not only wisely but graciously. I suffered with their characters but I also shared their triumphs! I sat on the fire escape (my skinny legs swinging over the bars) and read my favorite stories over and over. The apartment at 219

Bainbridge Street in Brooklyn, New York, was a refuge from the agony I witnessed in the streets.

I believed that all there was to know, of value, existed in books. Reading was my whole life.

Sharon Bell Mathis

Sharon Bell Mathis

John T. Whitney

When I was a boy I read with a passion, the same passion I had for food and games. Reading, I would say, came after food, and before games. I loved reading. I loved books and libraries, and the feel and smell of books. I still love to sniff new books. (Is that what they mean by the expression "getting high on books"?) I had a passion for books. I loved rainy-day vacations when there was nothing else pulling me, and I could give myself completely to reading.

It bothered my father that I spent so much time lying on my bed, reading and eating, with the book on the floor, my hand absently reaching for an apple or banana. The light was always too dim for my father. "You'll ruin your eyes reading like that," he said. "You read too much anyway. It's better to read less and understand what you're reading."

It's true I gobbled up books. When I came from the library, my arms bulged with books. I read whole shelves of books, or so it seemed to me: the entire *Rover Boys* series, then the *Tom Swifts*, then Jules Verne's books, and all of Mark Twain, in green bindings, and Charles Dickens in maroon. I liked authors who had written a lot of books. If possible I read them in order from the first book to the last. I read thin books and fat books. The size of a book never daunted me. I plunged into Tolstoy's bulky *War and Peace*. I read only for story. My eyes skidded over lengthy descriptions and philosophical ruminations. It's only as I grew older that I became interested in meaning and symbolism and the realistic treatment of character. What I remember from *The Adventures of Huckleberry Finn* was Huck in his father's grip, Huck imprisoned in a shack in the woods. In *The Adventures of Tom Sawyer* I remember how he was found out when he was disguised as a girl. I could hardly breathe when he was trapped in the cave. It took all my strength not to skip straight to the end. My eyes leaped ahead. I couldn't stop till I knew he and Becky were safe.

It was a wonderful way to read. Like hunger, nothing else mattered but that piece of bread. It wasn't literature I craved but action, conflict, suspense.

I still love books (still sniff them) but no more with that hunger and concentration I felt as a boy. I miss that passion, the grip of the story. I'm happy when I see it in children, that rapt attention, the ability to lock out everything but the story. I see the story reflected in those children's faces. The memories of those faces give purpose and meaning to everything I do.

Harry Mazer

Harry Mazer

The poet, Paul Zweig, writing about storytelling, said, "...all stories...beckon us out of the visible....The story is like wind filtering through cracks in a wall: it gives evidence of the vastness."

Poets often say what the rest of us only blunder at. Zweig's remarks describe more fully than I can the spirit of those hours of my childhood spent reading: absorbed, immersed, *beckoned*. Caught up in a story, I was beyond the present, beyond my mother's calls, my sisters' teasing. I was, in all but body, *somewhere else*.

To hear a story, to read a story, to be transported *somewhere else* is surely one of the basic human joys. I remember walking to school reading a book because I couldn't bear to wait all day to find out what happened next. I not only read walking *to* school, and *after* school, and at night after the lights were turned out and I was supposedly asleep (but really huddled under the covers with a book and a flashlight), but *in* school, my book of the moment inside my textbook. I read a great many books of all kinds. As long as it was between covers and had a story, I read it. So, to pare down my list of books which made a great impression on me to only three is difficult, but here goes:

The *Nancy Drew* series

There's no use picking out a single Nancy Drew title. It's all or nothing. At the right time in my life, when I was about ten years old, I was hooked on Nancy Drew. *The Mystery of the Winding Staircase. The Secret in the Old Clock.* What marvelous titles! (And Nancy and Ned— what a perfect pair. Even better than Ken and Barbie.) You read *Nancy Drew* books the way you eat popcorn—once you get started, you can't stop.

Gulliver's Travels

I read Gulliver for pure fun when I was growing up. It had a *story*— that's what counted. Then I read it again when I was older, and it was even better; there was story, and there were all the things Swift was saying in his sly, wry manner. *Gulliver's Adventures in Lilliput* are the best, of course, but if you're a little bit patient, his other adventures are also terrific. If you can find an old, illustrated hardbound copy, you're way ahead of the game. (I'm so sorry that, today, only books for the very young are illustrated.) I can still see Gulliver standing on the palm of the lovely queen of the land of Brobdingnagians.

The Diary of Anne Frank
    A book I will always cherish. Read this—you'll come to know Anne so well, and to find her so much like yourself in her heart that, at the end, when you realize afresh that she really lived, and then died, before she had ever *really* lived, in a German concentration camp, you'll cry. I did.

Norma Fox Mazer

Ruth Putter

Anne McCaffrey

It is difficult for me to pick just three authors and/or books since I have always been an avid reader. (If one is a writer, one is also a great reader: one never knows when some information one reads may be of use in a novel).

I remember most clearly my mother reading to my brothers and me from Rudyard Kipling's *Just So Stories*, the Mowgli yarns, and I still reread his classic *Kim* for the sheer pleasure of his storytelling genius. Since he can be enjoyed, as an author, by any age, I would put him at the top of my list.

When I was about ten, my mother also suggested I read A. Merritt's *The Ship of Ishtar*, then a serial in "Argosy" magazine. I devoured any of Mr. Merritt's books I could find. You might say that between Kipling and Merritt the groundwork was laid for my fascination with science fiction and science fantasy.

Of even more lasting significance was my discovery of Austin Tappan Wright's *Islandia* which I read at fourteen. This meticulously developed "other continent on our planet" influenced me more than any other single book. It was, alas, his only published work. I have bought, and passed on to friends, at least twenty hardcovers and paperbacks—and now hide one from myself so that when I wish to reread it, I have a copy available. Mr. Wright's philosophy of life did much to form my own.

Anne McCaffrey

Anne McCaffrey

Tara Heinemann

United States Senate
WASHINGTON, D.C. 20510

By the time I was through the first four grades at the old wooden Whittier School and had advanced to Central—the brick complex which housed the fifth through the ninth grades—I had become a frequent visitor to Mitchell's Carnegie Library. That building, constructed of ageless Sioux Falls granite, held a fascination for me that grew with the years. Several times a week I would browse through the aisles. A cozy reading room was equipped with oak tables and chairs. Frequently after school or on Saturdays I went to that room to dig up facts for a school paper. During the long summer vacation months, that library was my treasured and unfailing friend.

The first books I recall borrowing from the library were a series of animal adventure stories, including *Reddy the Fox* and *Bowser the Hound*. Those books brought animals to a human dimension in my mind. Then came two highlights of my reading endeavors—Mark Twain's *The Adventures of Tom Sawyer* and *The Adventures of Huckleberry Finn*. I raced through those books with delight and wonderment. That experience was one of the lasting joys of my boyhood.

The Altsheler series held my attention for at least two summers. These books of the American frontier, Indian scouts, hunters, trappers, and backwoodsmen fired my imagination and curiosity about life in the American West.

In my later years, books were to influence the course of my life. I became a compulsive reader. It has always been important to me to have a book at my bedside, in hotel rooms, on airplanes or trains, and on vacation. I am sure that you will find books to be among your best of friends, and among your best of times.

George McGovern

My earliest recollection of reading was right along with my mother as she read Walt Disney comic books to my brother and me. There were also some wonderful little story books with fabulous pictures of ants and their life in matchbox beds with soda-top tables and firefly lamps.

My next reading rampage (and it was that!) was all of the *Nancy Drew* mysteries. I read and reread *all* of them for years...so exciting...such fun, and she solved them all on her own!

Then came *Cyrano de Bergerac*. What a beautiful play! Love, passion, and desire soared through my veins at age thirteen, so thrilled was I by the language. I never dreamed simple words could evoke such emotion. I imagine reading that play set my course for the career I follow now. Thank you! Thank you, Edmond Rostand.

Lee Meriwether

Lee Meriwether

I still have many of the books that I loved as a child. When I see them on my shelf I remember the pleasure of kicking off my shoes and curling up on the couch with an apple in one hand and a book in the other. Here are three books I read over and over:

Little Women by Louisa May Alcott

To an only child like me, stories about large families were always interesting, but the Marches were special because they seemed so *real*. I identified most with slapdash Jo, but I yearned to be like all the girls: calm as Meg, beautiful as Amy, noble as Beth. They seemed almost as close as sisters to me.

This Singing World edited by Louis Untermeyer

I loved to read poetry when I was a child, and this collection was especially satisfying because it had a big section of funny verse. When I look through the book now I'm surprised at how many of the poems in it I know by heart. I never meant to memorize them—they just stuck in my head as I read them over and over.

The Good Master by Kate Seredy

My fifth-grade teacher read aloud this story about life on a Hungarian farm, and afterwards I read it to myself many times. It had beautiful pictures, and the girl in the story was as spunky and adventurous as I would have liked to be.

Betty Miles

Betty Miles

Authors I read between the age of eleven through thirteen:

Mark Twain
Exciting characterizations. Wonderful humor and touching relationships between the people he wrote about.

Jack London
High adventure and drama. Stories about people and parts of the world I had never read about before.

Agatha Christie
Lots of fun trying to solve the mystery before the end of the book.

Nicholasa Mohr

Nicholasa Mohr

Gail Russell

THE VICE PRESIDENT

WASHINGTON

While it is too difficult to single out a favorite book or author that I had during my childhood, I certainly do recall the many hours I spent in reading for pleasure. I continue to read as much as I can, even though my duties as Vice President require great amounts of reading. I enjoy history books most of all, as I did while I was growing up. I certainly hope that youngsters today will read not only in school, but at home. It is the best way to learn more about the world, the people in it, and how we all can work together to accomplish our goals.

Walter F. Mondale

Ricardo Montalbán

The three books that have had the greatest impression on me since young adulthood are:

Don Quixote by Cervantes

The Works of Shakespeare

My constant companion through life, the Bible

Ricardo Montalbán

Ricardo Montalbán

125

Books have always played a central role in my life. It's really difficult to pinpoint which books have had the greatest influence or effect, but some stand out for particular reasons and seem, at this sitting, appropriate.

I came across *Laughing to Keep from Crying* by Langston Hughes at a point in my life when I thought all writers were white and the subject of any book had to be far removed from my own experiences. The stories of Langston Hughes put this myth aside and introduced me to a joyous style of writing which I have loved since first reading the book. Hughes had treated the Black experience with a style and dignity which I had felt, and he had done so without resorting to a literature of rage.

The *Rime of the Ancient Mariner* by Samuel Taylor Coleridge was interesting from two aspects. My ninth-grade class acted out the entire piece, demonstrating the interplay between narrative, dialogue, and what I considered to be poetic effect, in a way that made the writing live for me. Then, at eighteen, I found myself sailing in the same waters that the author had visited (off the coasts of Newfoundland and Nova Scotia) and many of the "effects" of the piece turned out to be accurate descriptions of natural phenomena, making the rereading a particular pleasure.

Penguin Island by Anatole France was also introduced to me by a teacher. That France, a Nobel prize winner, had approached his subject in such a whimsical manner was fascinating. But when the author used his penguin-people to explore a host of serious concepts, the book became absolutely enthralling. Although I did not agree with all of France's ideas, it opened up many creative possibilities to me that had not seemed possible before.

Other books, naturally, have had other effects on my life. These three, however, seemed to have extended my possibilities as a writer more than most.

Walter Dean Myers

E. Algonaldo Thomas

BOB NEWHART

When I was a child I must have been one of the most avid readers of Sherlock Holmes. I couldn't wait to finish one book so I could start again on the next. I can't think of any of his books I haven't read.

The two other authors I read that I think probably influenced my decision to go into comedy were Robert Benchley, again almost all his books, and almost all of the books of Max Shulman.

Bob Newhart

Bob Newhart

Stover at Yale by Owen Johnson

Going to college in the 1930s was not taken for granted. For many of us, it was a venture into the unknown. *Stover at Yale,* a delightful book, gave me some idea of how young men ought to conduct themselves in college, that is, that they should be slightly eccentric, good-natured, frequently in agony over girls and over examinations, and not loners, but part of a group.

You Know Me, Al by Ring Lardner

This was my introduction to the works of Lardner, which I went on to enjoy for decades. It helped me to understand the use of satire, and showed me an approach to sports writing which took athletes out of the usual heroic mold.

The Robber Barons by Matthew Josephson

This was a muckraking, debunking account of how great American fortunes were made. It was disillusioning for a teenager, and it must have been challengeable in places, but it made the point that things are not necessarily what they seem, and that skepticism is advisable. This last was an essential truth for anyone going into the news business.

Edwin Newman

ANDRE NORTON

It is difficult at my age to look back through so many years and so many thousands of books read to pick out only three titles. As a child I was an avid reader and went through any book which came to hand. I went to the library once a week and, since we were limited to only two books at a time then, I chanced upon—to my great joy—shelves of the bound copies of the "St. Nicholas" magazine which were the answer to my problem as two of such gave me a number of serials as well as short stories.

The *Uncle Wiggily* stories were my delight when I was preschool, and I had almost a full set of them. I liked to believe that animals lived as do people—in fact all my life I have been able to enjoy companionship with animals, and I believe that my sensitivity to their helplessness was fostered by this early love of such stories.

However, my greatest love—and I still often reread them today— were the *Oz* books. I have never been able to understand the odd blind spot in librarians (and I was one for twenty years) which led many to condemn these books—they are the only truly American fairy tales. *The Land of Oz* and *Dorothy and the Wizard in Oz* were my first favorites.

Perhaps Burnett's *The Little Princess* was my next treasure which I read over and over again.

When I reached high school the *John Carter* stories by Burroughs (I never did like Tarzan very much) opened a whole new world of imagination for me—I had not been aware that that existed before though I had always longed to find such tales.

As I say, I have been a great reader always, but the writers I enjoyed the most as I came into my teens included Talbot Mundy and Dornford Yates—both of whom I can still read with pleasure.

Andre Norton

The book that I loved most as a child was *The Mowgli Stories* by Rudyard Kipling. Mowgli was a jungle boy who was raised by wolves.

This is what I would like to say to children today:

Read for escape, read for adventure, read for romance, but read the great writers. You will find to your delight that they are easier and more joy to read than the second-rate ones. They touch your imagination and your deepest yearnings, and when your imagination is stirred it can lead you down paths you never dreamed you would travel. If you read great language you will develop, without your realizing it, an appreciation of excellence that can shape your life.

Read Edgar Allan Poe, Jack London, Jules Verne, Ernest Hemingway. And read poetry—in whatever anthology your school gives you. Rhythm is what should first seize you when you read poetry. Do you know "The Congo" by Vachel Lindsay, "Tarantella" by Alfred Noyes? Read Countee Cullen, e. e. cummings, Emily Dickinson, Siegfried Sassoon. Do you know "The Fog" by Carl Sandburg? It is modelled on the Japanese haiku which is only allowed to be seventeen syllables long and doesn't have to rhyme. You could try to write a poem like that.

If you read, you may want to write. Great painters learned to paint by copying Old Masters in museums. You can learn to write by trying to copy the writers you like. Writing helps you to express your deepest feelings. Once you can express yourself you can tell the world what you want from it or how you would like to change it. All the changes in the world, for good or evil, were first brought about by words.

Jacqueline Kennedy Onassis

Jacqueline Kennedy Onassis

camera 5 inc.

The Arabian Nights

For a long time these were the only stories I enjoyed reading. Rich in imagination and conjuring up wonderful images in my mind, whilst the story line held my interest throughout. I always had, and now looking back I'm very pleased that I *did* have, a fertile imagination and these stories, along with Malory's tales from *King Arthur and His Knights*, helped to develop that imagination.

A Christmas Carol by Charles Dickens

To tell the truth I always resisted many worthy attempts to get me to read *David Copperfield* at the age of three. In England at any rate there was a tendency to force "improving" novels like Dickens' and Austen's works onto children who found the language difficult. But *A Christmas Carol* is a shorter and simpler story. It has ghosts in it which I always found a great plus in any stories. But it contains in it all that I've grown to love about Dickens. His superb descriptions of a time and a place and a way of life, and his honest, straightforward love of humanity which comes across so loud and clear that it's like having a favourite uncle sitting beside you telling you tales. A lovely book which I reread every Christmas. It gets better and better.

The Journals of Captain Scott's Polar Journey

Scott's own diaries of the expedition which ended in his death. I was fascinated by tales of exploration, of men facing something totally unknown—whether it was Hudson trapped by polar ice in a small wooden boat or Livingstone or Fawcett in the jungle. But Scott's journals, besides having all the narrative excitement of an expedition which was fighting against time to become the first to reach the South

Pole, and besides all its geographical and scientific curiosity, are in the end a very, very moving account of men coming to terms with an inevitable death. They're written clearly and simply and I know of nothing else in literature which moves me so much as the final few entries. Absorbing stuff on every level.

Well, those are three books. There were many more. I loved reading and I think that the wide variety of tales and stories and diaries and biographies which I read in my first eighteen years really helped to develop my own talents as a writer and above all my tolerance towards people and my enjoyment of the infinite differences between us all.

Michael Palin

Charles H. Percy

𝔘𝔫𝔦𝔱𝔢𝔡 𝔖𝔱𝔞𝔱𝔢𝔰 𝔖𝔢𝔫𝔞𝔱𝔢

COMMITTEE ON
GOVERNMENTAL AFFAIRS
WASHINGTON, D.C. 20510

The Autobiography of Benjamin Franklin is the first book that comes to mind. The youthful struggle of this great man, the depth of his knowledge and understanding that came through self-education, his philosophical as well as mechanical and electrical aptitude, his grasp of government as well as all issues affecting his fellow man, and his sense of compassion and understanding as well as his hard-headed approach to life, provided a great source of inspiration to me.

Black Beauty was a book that gripped me emotionally and made me sensitive to all animals. As a city boy who had been raised all my life in the city and only knew a horse because it was in front of an ice wagon or milk wagon, *Black Beauty* took me into areas that I was never able to visit as a child and made me sensitive to the needs of all members of the animal kingdom.

The *Tom Swift* books, the entire series, every one that was written at the time of my childhood, provided a source of great fascination to me. It brought me into the world of mechanical development, new ideas and inventiveness. In a Walter Mitty sense, I could enjoy vicariously the pleasures of life through the eyes of Tom Swift.

Charles H. Percy
United States Senator

Ann Petry

The Ugly Duckling by Hans Christian Andersen

Little Women by Louisa May Alcott

The Moonstone by Wilkie Collins

I grew up in a small town in New England. The winters were long
and cold and dark set in early. My mother used to read aloud to us —
usually *Grimm's Fairy Tales,* and *Andersen's Fairy Tales.* Her voice
transported us out of that bleak environment into a world of magic,
filled with animals who talked, wicked stepmothers, enchanted
princesses, dwarves, lost children. Of all these stories my favorite was
"The Ugly Duckling" — the story of the drab, rejected misfit who
discovers that he is a swan, "the most beautiful of all beautiful birds."

I became a full-fledged reader when someone gave me *Little Women*
and I discovered Jo March, the tomboy, the misfit, the impatient quick-
tempered, would-be writer. I felt as though she was part of me and I
was part of her despite the fact that she was white and I was black.
Occasionally she "felt rumpled up in her mind" and so did I.
Sometimes she said things like "I wish I was a horse then I could run for
miles in this splendid air, and not lose my breath." And so did I.

I was eleven years old when I read Wilkie Collins' *The Moonstone* —
that intricately plotted story about the theft of an enormous yellow
diamond (the moonstone) from the head of an idol known as the
moon-god. This occurred in India in 1799. The search for the stolen

diamond takes place in England in the mid-nineteenth century. It involves faithful servants, inept aristocrats, a clairvoyant child, Indian jugglers, and, of course, the great Sergeant Cuff: "When it comes to unravelling a mystery there isn't the equal in England of Sergeant Cuff." There still isn't.

The Moonstone served as my introduction to the world of books written for adults and it turned me into an omnivorous reader.

Ann Petry

The Lion, the Witch and the Wardrobe by C. S. Lewis

Chronicles of Narnia by C. S. Lewis

The Little Prince by Antoine de Saint-Exupéry

Mackenzie Phillips

As a youth, *Aesop's Fables* and "The Ugly Duckling" made a great impression on me. Luckily, I grew up with a mother who read to me constantly, as I do with my own seven-year-old. Consequently he is also very proficient at reading.

As a young teenager, *The Robe* by Lloyd C. Douglas was so important that I read and reread it immediately.

I cannot imagine a life without books! Please try and read. It is so important to our education.

Juliet Prowse

CBS NEWS

The stories of Rudyard Kipling

Introduction to Physics (Author unknown. This particular book was used as a standard textbook at Reagan High School, Houston, Texas, in the very late 1940s.)

Coronado's Children by J. Frank Dobie

My mother read aloud to me Kipling and Dobie. That, in itself, led to their making impressions upon me at a very early age (preschool and on into early school.) I remember loving the sense of adventure in Kipling's stories, and remember being taught lessons of courage and self-reliance from them. The Dobie book gave me an early sense of history and a feeling for my heritage: Rather and Page families (Page was my mother's maiden name), Texas, and America. While I was never a good science student, the physics book sparked a lifetime interest in science and drove home the fact that no person can hope to be considered educated wihout some scientific study.

Dan Rather

JOAN RIVERS

My favorite books as a child were *The Secret Garden, Mary Poppins,* and all the *Nancy Drew* mysteries.

Joan Rivers

ORAL ROBERTS

I cannot mention three specific books, but rather three series of books.

My seventh grade grammar books

My history books in all my growing years

Jack London's books of fiction—*The Call of the Wild* and *White Fang* are strong in my memory.

You ask me why? In the seventh grade my English teacher made grammar live for me. I've grown in English since, but seventh grade rooted me in the desire to learn to speak and write good English.

History has always fascinated me as I am interested in people more than any other force.

Fiction gave wings to my dreams, and Jack London's books about the far north started me on a life of reading.

Oral Roberts

Oral Roberts

A Child's Garden of Verse by Robert Louis Stevenson

Up from Slavery by Booker T. Washington

A Tale of Two Cities by Charles Dickens

Roxie Roker

Books had a profound affect on me as I was growing up, and over the years I have accumulated a rather large library! Some of my favorites are:

The *Babar* books of Jean and Laurent de Brunhoff. I identify strongly with the character of Zephir, the monkey, and appreciate his inquisitive spirit.

The Little Prince by Antoine de Saint-Exupéry taught me much about what is important though invisible.

The books of Constantin Stanislavski, especially *An Actor Prepares*, sustained my belief in the possibility of a creative life.

May the GOOD NEWS be yours!

Richard Sander
a.k.a. Les Nessman

Little Women

The Bobbsey Twins

The Legend of Sleepy Hollow

Isabel Sanford

The Graduate School and University Center
of the City University of New York

Mark Twain, especially *The Adventures of Tom Sawyer, The Adventures of Huckleberry Finn,* and *A Connecticut Yankee in King Arthur's Court*—because Mark Twain is the most American of writers, the "Lincoln of our literature," as Howells called him, and because he is a marvelous storyteller.

Two novelists who gave me an early and abiding passion for history—the now forgotten British writer of boy's books, G. A. Henty, and, when I was a little older, the unforgettable French romancer, Alexandre Dumas, especially the D'Artagnan series and *The Count of Monte Cristo.*

Two writers who showed me the infinite excitement of the future—Jules Verne and H. G. Wells.

And how can I omit Robert Louis Stevenson, especially *Treasure*

Island, The Strange Case of Dr. Jekyll and Mr. Hyde, and *The New Arabian Nights?*

As for the children of today, I can only urge you to read all the books you can while you are young—because you will live the rest of your life off the reading you did before you were twenty.

Arthur Schlesinger, Jr.

Gretchen Stewart

CHARLES M. SCHULZ

When I was a teenager, the three books that gave me the most enjoyment and probably led me on to more reading were the Sherlock Holmes stories, *Beau Geste,* and *Ivanhoe.*

I also read every comic magazine and *Big Little Book* that came out.

Charles M. Schulz

Charles M. Schulz

First and foremost, I read comic books. All kinds (Batman, Donald Duck, war comics, westerns, and sports comics), and as often as possible. Kept a large collection, and reread them constantly, particularly during breakfast and lunch—a habit encouraged by my mother. (Reading at the dinner table, when the entire family was gathered, was not allowed.) Aside from learning to enjoy quick-paced adventure stories, reading comics—and rereading them—helped develop my reading speed considerably, which was a big help from then on. (For the same reasons, and for the simple reason to encourage the habit of reading, I've aided and abetted my son's comic book hobby.)

By the time I was fourteen, I was working in both the school library during part of the school day, and in a nearby public library after school. So, trying to pin down two or three books I read during that time is difficult at best.

But I do remember enjoying some of Howard Pease's adventures involving young boys who managed to get a job on a freighter/tanker and found mystery and excitement at sea. Later, I remember going on a Steinbeck binge and reading just about everything he wrote. But then, at that age, I read a little of everything—and if I liked one book by an author, I read his (or her) others.

Dewey Schurman

I had many favorite books when I was a child—it is hard to pick only three! But I will try. When I was very small I loved "The Story of Chicken Little" and Robert Louis Stevenson's *A Child's Garden of Verse*. And in school I read and reread *Toby Tyler* and *Pinocchio in Africa*. And my own first book was Mark Twain's *The Prince and the Pauper*. But then I mustn't forget *Mickey Mouse in Pygmyland*, *Alice in Wonderland*, and my very favorite, George MacDonald's *The Princess and the Goblin*.

Well, I told you it was too hard to pick only three!

I have no photograph of myself—so here is a self-portrait.

Maurice Sendak

DESERT,INN
and Country Club

Looking back, I think the three books I enjoyed most are ones that not only were enjoyable to me as a youngster, but also ones that I enjoyed reading over and over even today. These three are:

The Adventures of Tom Sawyer by Mark Twain

The Adventures of Huckleberry Finn by Mark Twain

The Red Badge of Courage by Stephen Crane

I can remember reading these books, and being filled with a tremendous feeling of adventure, almost as if I were right there along with Tom and Huck. I'm sure that anyone who reads these great books will also experience the same exciting sensation. What a fantastic way to let your imagination take you on adventures that you can relive always!

Lonnie

Lonnie Shorr

Neil Simon

The three books and authors which made the greatest impression on me as a child were:

The Adventures of Huckleberry Finn by Mark Twain

Great Expectations by Charles Dickens

Northwest Passage by Kenneth Louis Roberts

Neil Simon

F R A N K   S I N A T R A

Probably the book which moved me most was *Dr. Hudson's Secret Journal*. Fortunately, I found it at a very early age and continue rereading it even now. I recommend it most highly to young people everywhere because of the great message of hope and goodness it imparts. Without getting deeply into it, I would merely tell you that *The Secret Journal of Dr. Hudson* deals with acts of kindness to our fellow men and women. Acts which lose some of their value once they are known. The philosophy is one which we could use more in the world today—that of enriching our own lives by helping others without necessarily their knowledge or the knowledge of any other living souls. A great book.

My second choice would be Walter B. Pitkin's *Psychology of Achievement*, which came to my attention when I was fourteen years of age. When I first read it I didn't even understand it all. I don't know that I do today. But I assure you it is a beacon of light to ambition and the quality of one's life. Briefly, Mr. Pitkin points out that any of us may have hundreds of successes in our lives and yet never achieve. The man who is broke, needs money desperately and wins what he needs in a poker game Friday night has by so doing enjoyed a success. He has achieved nothing.

Mr. Pitkin pushes his readers into making achievement their goal instead of success. Finally, he defines an achievement as a series of distinguished, successful endeavors usually in the face of difficulty. A great book. Difficult to read and most difficult to comprehend fully. But a great book.

As a third choice, rather than name a specific book I would suggest all youngsters read more biographies and, more importantly, autobiographies. I have never spent much time reading novels which in their finest form are fiction. They are stories created for the novel form. The majority are written in a make-believe world of manufactured people and contrived solutions to all problems and relationships. Biographies and autobiographies, on the other hand, lead us into a greater understanding of life as it has been lived. Of real problems that have been overcome by strength and faith and wisdom. In short, they deal with real life and since that's what we are all living I feel we should all be greater students of it.

Frank Sinatra

The Good Earth by Pearl S. Buck

The Pearl by John Steinbeck (adolescence)

The Prophet by Kahlil Gibran

The Jungle Books by Rudyard Kipling (early childhood)

Beatrix Potter books

Historical and pictorial books

Jan Smithers

The three books which made the deepest impression upon me when I was young are:

The Voyages of Doctor Doolittle by Hugh Lofting

Tarzan of the Apes by Edgar Rice Burroughs

South Wind by Norman Douglas

The Voyages of Doctor Doolittle was the first book I selected on my own and read all the way through. It and the others in the series were filled with humor and gentleness, and I was too innocent to be disturbed by the racial slurs that a later generation finds objectionable.

Tarzan of the Apes was the first book that kept me enthralled. I must have been nine or ten when I read it. Words that I did not understand I passed over shamelessly, for I was too eager to read on and couldn't stop to look into a dictionary. To this day, no superhero has replaced Tarzan. For me, he is the ultimate male.

South Wind bewitched me. I read it at the age of fourteen and discovered the majesty of prose. It was the first adult novel by a master storyteller that I had encountered, and I gasped with admiration. Language, I learned, could be magically beautiful and powerful. Now, forty years later, I recall little of that wonderland. But when my eyes first feasted upon it, *South Wind* seemed the finest achievement of mankind.

Donald J. Sobol

The Adventures of Huckleberry Finn by Mark Twain (for humor)

The Old Man and the Sea (for simplicity)

Anything by Edgar Allan Poe (for effect)

It is impossible for anyone to read too much.

Jim Stafford

Laddie books by Alfred Payson Terhune

Travel books by Richard Halliburton, especially his description of "The Blue Grotto" in Italy

All kinds of biographies of great people—especially musicians.

Jean Stapleton

Jean Stapleton

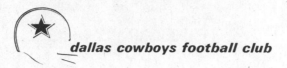

dallas cowboys football club

The ability to read and understand what I am reading has always been important to me. It is important because I wouldn't be able to function in the business world if I couldn't read. Also, one of my favorite pastimes is to read. I enjoy reading both fiction and nonfiction books and always have one close at hand.

Three books that I read when I was younger and left an impression with me were the autobiographies of Lou Gehrig, Bob Mathis, and George Washington Carver. recall the exact titles or authors, but the message in each one of these books has always impressed me.

These books contain stories of people who were able to meet the challenges they faced in life. It wasn't always easy for them and they often had uphill battles, but they did it. Reading these books taught me important qualities such as perseverance, dedication, loyalty, and hard work. And I have tried to incorporate these qualities into my life. They have helped me to be successful.

Read to learn and to enjoy.

Roger Staubach

CBS
ENTERTAINMENT

Ever since I can remember, I dreamed of becoming an actress. As a child, I eagerly read everything I could get my hands on about the subject. Three books which stand out in my mind as particularly helpful and inspirational were:

An Actor Prepares by Constantin Stanislavski

Building a Character by the same author

Acting: The First Six Lessons by Boleslavski.

Loretta Swit

I must be honest—when you ask me to list books I read in my childhood days, I must say *none*. All my reading was of newspapers (front to back), magazines, and comic books.

My interests were always in current events and sports.

I developed the "book reading habit" slightly as I got older—but—to this day, my reading is *still* basically newspapers and magazines.

Vic Tayback

Vic Tayback

Lee Trevino

My thanks to the children who chose to hear from the Super Mex. Unfortunately, when I was a youngster I did not have a great deal of reading material available to me. In this day and time it is almost a crime if a child does not do extensive reading. There are so many libraries filled with books about everything available now to almost anyone, that parents, along with children, should see to it that they have the opportunity that I did not have.

There are three books that I read during my childhood which I believe made a great impression on my life and career. The first one which was available to me was the Bible. Many things that I read in it then are still with me in my later years. The second book read by me that you could say changed my professional career was Ben Hogan's book *Five Lessons: The Fundamentals of Golf*. This book taught me to hit the golf ball from left to right. The third book was about the history of Texas. I think every child should read and learn about their home state so that they can be knowledgeable when asked questions pertaining to their respective home state.

Once again thank you for choosing me and if every child that reads this letter will read a book, I, for one, will be very gratified.

Lee Trevino

BROADCASTING SYSTEM, INC.

The three books that were most impressive to me during my childhood were:

The Deerslayer

For Whom the Bell Tolls

Mutiny On the Bounty

Reading has always been a pleasurable activity for me and in college I was a student of the humanities. Reading now is mostly confined to business, but I still recall with pleasure the enjoyment of the above-mentioned books.

R. E. Turner

steven tyler

During my early childhood, the rhyme, "Over in the Meadow" by Ezra Keats was my favorite piece. My mother believes to this day that the rhythm and story affected my start in music.

The Boy Who Discovered the Earth, and I cannot recall the author, was my next favorite.

Finally, John Steinbeck's *Travels With Charley*, I still think of as the book which I enjoyed the most. It gave me the lasting desire to travel and make the most out of life.

Steven Tyler

LEON URIS

Two of the books that made the heaviest impact on me as a youngster were John Steinbeck's *Tortilla Flat* and Howard Fast's *Citizen Tom Paine*.

I loved John Steinbeck as a humanist, a fighter for social justice, and a writer who put the needs of others ahead of his own. *Tortilla Flat* to me was the most tender and compassionate story of the underdog that I had ever read and had a marked influence on my own career.

In *Tom Paine* my eyes were opened to a dissident who dared to take unpopular views at a time when it was exceedingly dangerous to do so. He represents another thing I love about writers, the maverick element, the courage to swim upstream.

Finally, my third selection does not exactly conform to your question, but I feel it is relevant to what you are trying to say. I flunked English a number of times, and one year in my sophomore or junior year I had to go to summer school. It was then a teacher opened my eyes to Shakespeare and gave life to the language in a way that I had never known. Funny I don't even remember the man's name, but I remember his face.

Leon Uris

Dear Abby

I read both for information and pleasure, and the following books made a great impression on me:

The Human Mind by Karl Menninger
   (Even as a young lay person it gave me much information about why people behave as they do.)

Lust for Life by Irving Stone
   (Gave me an insight into the life of a genius . . . Van Gogh.)

For Whom the Bell Tolls by Ernest Hemingway
   (Was sheer entertainment as well as an example of how a classic should be written. When I read it I had no idea that it would become a classic piece of literature.)

Abigail Van Buren

Abigail Van Buren

Ala Moana
Americana

It's easy for me to list my three most enjoyable books. Unfortunately, I do not remember the authors. However, the books were:

Nobody's Boy
   I think it took place in France so it may have been a French author.

The Secret Garden

The Smuggler's Sloop

Dick Van Patten

Dick Van Patten

P.S. I believe I was between ten and fourteen when I read these books.

Hervé Villechaize

Uncle Tom's Cabin

Twenty Thousand Leagues under the Sea

Around the World in Eighty Days

   —or any books written by Jack London or Jules Verne.

The books that made the greatest impression on me in my childhood were fairy tale books—all those wonderful Blue, Red, Green, Yellow, etc. collections. The day I went to my library and discovered I had read every one in the place, I cried.

Judith Viorst

Milton Viorst

Catcher in the Rye by J. D. Salinger (early adolescence)

The Black Stallion (childhood)

The Day Lincoln Was Shot by Jim Bishop

   Also: *Pictorial History of World War I and World War II* (multi-volume set)

Robert Walden

December 12. Inc.

My favorite childhood authors were:

Charlotte Brontë
Charles Dickens
Henry Wadsworth Longfellow

Reading is the key to knowledge, achievement, and success.

Dionne Warwick

Harry Langdon Photography

𝕌nited 𝕊tates 𝕊enate

SENATOR LOWELL WEICKER

The short stories of Guy DeMaupassant

The short stories of Bret Harte

The Kenneth Roberts books

Paul M. Barrett

Paul M. Barrett
Press Aide

PHYLLIS A. WHITNEY

I have been asked to tell you a little about the reading I did when I was young. Growing up in the Orient, with no radio or television, and not even any movies to speak of, I began reading very young. Books became my greatest source of entertainment. And they were my consolation too, when I was lonely.

They still are. While I enjoy television at times, there is nothing that can take the place of a book. In a book I can *live* the story and get inside the thoughts of the hero or heroine. It's not just watching—it is taking part in the characters' problems, and living in places I might never see, being with people whom I might never otherwise meet.

Since I may only give you three titles that I enjoyed, it is hard to choose. I enjoyed all the Oz books because they set my imagination soaring. When I was a little older, my favorite book was *The Secret Garden* by Frances Hodgson Burnett. I liked the girl in that story because she wasn't especially nice. She could behave very badly, yet she grew and learned and turned out very well in the end. I don't think I've ever met a hero I liked better than Dickon in *The Secret Garden*. This book introduced me to mystery for the first time and I began to make up stories of my own in my head.

Then when I was in my teens and was haunting libraries wherever I lived, I discovered Mary Roberts Rinehart. She may seem old-fashioned today, but again, her mystery novels inspired me and made me wonder if someday I would write a mystery story of my own.

It's good to be able to tell you that my story turned out well too— and I really did grow up to write those mystery novels myself!

Phyllis A. Whitney

Phyllis A. Whitney

Louis Manna

ANDY WILLIAMS

The following three books proved to leave a deep impression on me during my childhood and adolescence:

The Count of Monte Cristo

Alice Through the Looking Glass

Barnaby Rudge by Charles Dickens

Andy Williams

United States Senate

COMMITTEE ON LABOR AND
HUMAN RESOURCES
WASHINGTON, D.C. 20510

The books which made a great impression on me as a child were *The Adventures of Huckleberry Finn* by Mark Twain, the *Rover Boys* series by Edward Stratemayer, and the *Boy Allies* series by Clair Wallace Hayes.

These books were full of intrigue, and the plots were infused with a message. They sparked my imagination and set me to dreaming of daring exploits. The characters were adventurous and willing to try new things, and I was inspired by their achievements and their patriotism.

Harrison A. Williams, Jr.

Phyllis Anderson Wood

I've been asked to tell you the names of three books I read during my youth which made a great impression on me. Seems like a reasonable thing to ask an author, doesn't it? Well, if you weren't people I respect so highly, I might be tempted to put together a phony answer that would sound appropriate coming from an author. But I won't. Instead, I'll level with you just as you've so often leveled with me.

There simply aren't three books that made a heavy impression on me in my younger years. (It wasn't until much later that I started to do any reading for pleasure.) When I was young I used reading as a tool to learn things I wanted to know. It was useful but not memorable reading. In those years, if I had any spare time, I always preferred to sew or make things with my hands.

Actually, my reading habits have always been shaped by necessity. For years there was homework. And since then, professional reading and preparation of lessons. Even now, a novel is a luxury for me.

As I look back on it, I see that I was never exposed in school to an array of young adult novels such as you are today. I never had the experience of curling up with a fast-reading book I could finish in an afternoon. And I don't recall any books in which I really became involved emotionally with the characters.

Perhaps this is why it seems urgent to me now—both as an author and as a teacher—to do what no teacher ever did for me, to make reading a feeling-activity. I want young readers to get inside the characters in the books, to love and worry and rejoice and make decisions along with them. And I want the readers to feel enough success that they will return for more and more books.

I'm hoping you'll discover the world of books earlier in your lives than I did. These days it's easy to let the TV set take over, saying the words to you, telling you how to feel. But there's much more to you than that. Right within your own brain you have resources that can outdo TV—a giant screen, color, full stereo, a memory bank full of scenes, and your own private screening room. With this remarkable equipment you can pick up a book and begin to see it come to life in your own mind. Think of the additional channels your mental set can add to your life.

True, you can grow up without reading a lot of books. But why limit yourself? As you're growing, why not develop all the dimensions you can? My hope is that you will build for yourselves rich, full, and rewarding lives. As part of this, I hope you'll be readers.

Phyllis Anderson Wood

Phyllis Anderson Wood

P.S. Although I can't tell you of any early favorites, I can tell you of three from my later years.

In college I discovered Kahlil Gibran's *The Prophet.*
As a mother I became a great admirer of E. B. White's *Charlotte's Web.*
And as a teacher I love Jane Wagner's *J. T.*

LITTLE, BROWN and COMPANY
PUBLISHERS

Mark Twain made an enormous impression on me in my childhood. I still consider him the greatest American author. His comical masterworks, *The Adventures of Tom Sawyer* and *The Adventures of Huckleberry Finn*, gave wonderful pleasure to young readers, yet adults can admire them for different, deeper reasons.

Alexandre Dumas was a favorite when I was an adolescent reader, and I still enjoy his work. His books are clear and easy to read, and full of thrilling adventures and fascinating characters. *The Three Musketeers* and *The Count of Monte Cristo* are his best books; very long, but they don't seem long once you get into them!

In my early teens, I loved to read science and fantasy fiction. An enormous new literature in these fields has sprung up since then. Youngsters who want to develop their reading skills while enjoying themselves can't do much better than read science fiction. The author I liked best, H. G. Wells, is still considered a master in the field. His science fiction books that most impressed me were *The Invisible Man*, *The Time Machine*, and *The War of the Worlds*.

Eddie Bauer

Herman Wouk

Growing up as a Chinese-American in San Francisco, I found few books which dealt with my own experience. I lived in a predominantly black area but commuted by bus every day to a bilingual school in Chinatown. Stories set on farms or in suburbia or Midwestern small towns were less real to me than science fiction or fantasy. Science fiction and fantasy dealt with strategies of survival: people adapting to strange new lands and worlds, or some fantastic or alien creature adjusting to ours. Adapting to different environments and cultures happened each time I got on and off the bus.

When I was eleven, I always enjoyed Andre Norton's ability to conjure up other worlds; and the world in *Star Born* was one of my favorites. The struggling seashore colony, the friendship between the boy and the alien amphibian, and the strange ruins of an even earlier culture were woven together to create a basic vision—a vision which was at once tough and yet melancholy, for one world had to end for another to be born. For me, it was a "spellbinding" book in the fullest sense of the word.

When I was fifteen, Ray Bradbury was another favorite author, especially his *Martian Chronicles*, whch did more than describe Mars. The intoxicating images and phrases had a rich texture of their own. If creating a world was a magical act, then the author had to pay special attention to the language of the incantation.

Finally, there was Robert Heinlein, who showed me that there were different ways for the incantation to be sung. So many of his fine adventure stories were spun from the substance of a first-person narrator that it's difficult for me to select one, but I think it would have to be *Glory Road*. Its philosophical discussions were a bit dreary, but I still enjoy that precise and yet humorous voice which was used to sing its worlds into existence.

L. Yep

Laurence Yep

Francine Ann Yep

I have already appeared in print saying I read *no* books as a teenager because the books I wanted had not been written yet. If I was forced to remember under hypnosis I might admit having read:

Kon-Tiki
I remember it as being wonderfully exciting, the *Jaws* of its time.

Remembrance of Things Past
I remember some guy listening to strange sounds behind a door.

The Glass Mountain
I remember I was fifteen at the time and had tuberculosis, doing a two-year rest cure at Stony World Sanatorium.

I also remember reading some horror stories about monkeys who shoved lady's torsos up chimneys—and monkeys' jaws which inadvertently brought the dead back to somebody's front door to knock.

I'm afraid I always did enjoy a good scare.

Paul Zindel

Harper & Row, Publishers, Inc.

There are many books which were most important to me when I was young. One was *The Secret Garden* by Frances Hodgson Burnett. Anyone who reads my own work closely will find the influence it had on me. Another was *Heidi*. Here, the loneliness and yearning of the child was so strong. I used to read *Heidi* over and over again. My sister had given me the book and I remember one day my mother went to her and said, "What kind of book did you give that child? It makes her cry so much." I also loved Albert Terhune's dog stories. His stories and *A Dog of Flanders* may be the source of my past and present love for animals.

It's hard to select just these few books because there were so many I loved. Things that I might not admire so much today meant a great deal to me then and did influence me subconsciously. That is why I feel writing what children read is so important and why I hope all writers give them only the finest work they are capable of doing. Being able to read is one of the best things in everybody's life.

Charlotte Zolotow

TITLE INDEX

Title Index

Title Index

AUTHOR INDEX